KEEPIN' THE BEAT

The Musical Journey Continues

THE LEGACY

TEDDY ADAMS

PAGE PUBLISHING
Conneaut Lake, PA

First originally published by Page Publishing 2024

ISBN 979-8-89315-273-9 (pbk)
ISBN 979-8-89315-757-4 (hc)
ISBN 979-8-89315-272-2 (digital)

Printed in the United States of America

Dedication

This book, my second attempt of expression (*The Up of the Down Beat*, 2017), chronicling my journey as a jazz musician, is simply entitled *Keepin' the Beat* and is a continuation of the past and an update and personal legacy for the future.

The following individuals are greatly responsible for my attempt to express the profoundness of the great art form commonly referred to as jazz and its creators/disciples. The people listed below inspired, encouraged, supported, and respected my journey, and without them, this, my second endeavor, would not have been possible.

Me, my brothers Lonnie and Bobby

My brothers, Lonnie and Bobby (both deceased), were always there with encouragement and support. They were visibly very proud of my attempt to keep the music alive. My oldest brother, Lonnie, was the reason that I became interested in jazz. He played the tenor saxophone (my first instrument), and later, I switched to trombone. The saxophone had too many keys. Lonnie had already started playing gigs and practiced all the time. He could have been a very good musician had he not joined the Air Force and made it a career. I had already subconsciously memorized many of the licks and phrases that he practiced all the time.

Bobby, my younger brother, was my personal promoter. He was proud of what I did and was my right-hand man when I promoted or produced concerts, performances, etc. Any and every time I performed, I always knew he was going to be there, inspiring and beaming with pride. Both Lonnie and Bobby never denied me their presence and support whenever I performed.

Me and Samuel Truell (Mac, Spike)

My main man and childhood friend, Samuel Truell, aka Spike but always Mac to me because that's what his mama called him, was a definite inspiration. Even though I never told him, he was a childhood hero. He inspired me then and still inspires me now. It was Mac who demonstrated to me by his attitude, tenacity, confidence, and overall approach to life that a person can accomplish whatever he sets out to do no matter what challenges may exist.

Undeniably challenged from birth, Mac grew up in our neighborhood as an equal to all of his peers. Throughout our childhood and school years including college, Mac demanded respect and equal treatment. When I say that he was one of the fellows, that's exactly what I mean. He was an intricate part of everything that we did, and I mean everything, good, bad, and often unbelievable.

Upon graduating from college, he married, maintained a family, taught school, and later pursued and retired from a prestigious career with the US government. He is still one of my few best friends, and he still inspires me. I drew from him the confidence that I could be a good musician because he proved that if you wanted something, it was possible. I'm sure that either subconsciously or by example, I approached music with confidence and determination knowing that I could accomplish what I wanted to if I wanted to bad enough. Thanks, Mac.

My mentor Willie Draper

Last, but certainly not the least, my mentor, Willie Draper (featured in my first book, *The Up of the Down Beat*) or Scoop, as he was fondly called, more than anyone is responsible for my understanding of life and this profound art form commonly referred to as jazz. Thank you from the abyss of my heart and more.

Above all, the Almighty Creator and my family, always beside, behind, or in front of me.

What Is Jazz?

Jazz, because of its profoundness, infinity, creativity, and innateness, defies an explanation/definition. There are generalizations, elusions, opinions, and academic definitions of jazz, but none amply describe its essence. Not knowing or being given a definition does not affect its essence. The "Proof Is in the Pudding." Most listeners know it when they hear it without dealing with what it is. Definitions are academic. "Proof positive" is created and rendered by the performers as they express the art form.

Profound Conclusions

If you have to ask what jazz is you will never know. (Louis Armstrong)

I don't know and I don't care. (Charlie Mingus)

I don't know but I care. (Daniel "Big Black" Ray)

Definitions, opinions, and/or conclusions are personal, but one thing is undeniable: the art form commonly referred to as jazz is one of the most profound music art forms in existence and one of America's gifts to the world.

An Almost Befitting Conclusion

In 1987, the US Congress declared jazz a national treasure. That's only almost befitting because the art form commonly referred to as jazz is, beyond a doubt, an international treasure and should be recognized as such.

Contents

Foreword

The origin of improvised jazz is attributed to New Orleans, Louisianna, although embryonic beginnings can be traced back to the drums and voices of Africa and sequentially include various eras, i.e., field songs/hollers, spirituals, blues, ragtime/stride, and traditional. Subsequently, swing, bebop, post-bebop, avant-garde, fusion, smooth jazz, etc. were developed. It is believed that because New Orleans was the only slave location in America that did not forbid the slaves from playing the drums and allowed them to creatively express themselves at Congo Square on Sundays (their day of rest) served as a precursor to the art form presently referred to as jazz. Perhaps another reason for this premise is the more liberal approach to slavery that was practiced by the French slave owners. Of course, in addition to the drums, voices, and dancing, other instruments opened the door for creative expression.

The Gullah/Geechee culture of the low country, which peripherally includes the southern border of North Carolina and the northern border of Florida, is musically akin to the spirit and essence of New Orleans's music legacy, the greatest concentration being between Charleston and Beaufort, South Carolina, and Savannah and Sea Island, Georgia. Charleston and Savannah are often viewed as sister cities, and even more, the realization that the music climate in both cities was developed independently from New Orleans: in Charleston, the Jenkins Orphanage and, in Savannah, the brass bands and exposure to outside influence from sojourners passing through because it was a thoroughfare to and from the northeast coast. Also both cities are large seaport towns that attract performing artists from numerous cities and countries. Dr. Charles Elmore's book, *All That Savannah Jazz*, is an ideal source for Savannah's exposure and contributions to music with an emphasis on jazz.

The journey of professional musician Teddy Adams is a continuation of his first book, *The Up of the Down Beat*. The material and information included in this book are an extension of some of those covered in his aforementioned first book and also share more recent experiences and revelations. The present posture of his life is interwoven with his past and focuses on the people, places, events, and experiences that enabled his journey to be a rewarding, enlightening, and sometimes regretful travel throughout life.

Special attention is given to the importance of the southern United States' contribution to the art form of jazz. Teddy Adams' inspiration, motivation, and understanding of the art form of jazz are derived from his hometown and other regional locations. The influence from his upbringing in Savannah, Georgia, and other cities in its vicinity amply prepared him for his musical journey throughout his life. He considers that as being one of his greatest blessings.

Acknowledgments

The following individuals and entities are a part of my musical journey and have my humble appreciation for supporting me and my efforts to contribute and perpetuate this great art form called jazz. In my opinion, it is the most profound music art form in existence and America's gift to the world.

- The musicians who recognized my potential and tolerated and taught me the truth about this art form. There were many but two in particular: Willie "Scoop" Draper and Varnell "Val" Davis.
- Savannah Jazz.
- The City of Savannah, for designating me as its first Official Ambassador of Jazz.
- My loyal and supportive fans and friends.
- Good Times Jazz Bar and Restaurant (Stephen and Danielle Moore, Chef Joe Randall).
- Juanita Adams, for editing assistance.
- L. B. Hood (*Hebrew Preacher*), for the cover artwork.
- My granddaughter, Thailer Ruby Fox, for her imaginative drawing of me as a child trombonist and the conga player.
- Beverly Worlds, for preparing the original manuscript for this book.
- The Eric Jones Trio (Eric Jones, Marc Chesanow, Robert Saunders), for their support and accompaniment on numerous music projects, etc. that I have done.

Hometown and Regional History/Entities/Venues

There has always been a jazz presence in Savannah and other neighboring areas, even when it was not fully appreciated or supported. Dr. Charles Elmore's book, *All that Savannah Jazz*, documents Savannah's jazz posture dating back to the early part of the twentieth century. This writer can testify to its presence from the early 1950s to the present. The following is a listing of clubs, venues, events, and entities that focused and helped perpetuate jazz for many years and in some instances still exist:

Adagio Jazz Club
Amvet's Night Club
Annabell's Night Club
Annual Christmas Concert and Jam Session
Bennie's Supper Club
Black Heritage Festival
Bop City Jazz Club
Captain Sam's River Boats
The Carousel Lounge
Coconut Grove Night Club
The Den Lounge
The Flamingo Club
Good Times Jazz Bar and Restaurant
Gunnie's Tremont Inn Club
Gus' Lounge

Hannah's East Jazz Club
Hard Hearted Hannah's Jazz Club
Joe's Blue Room
Joe Louis' After Hour Club
Johnny Harris Restaurant
LaCortier Lounge
The Looking Glass Lounge
The Marine Club
The Night Flight Night Club
Pappy's Lounge
Pete City Jazz Club
Post 500 VFW Club
Porter's 541 Lounge
Riviera Club
Ruby's 2 Spot Night Club
Savannah Arts Academy High School
Savannah Country Day School
Savannah Jazz Association (formerly Coastal Jazz Association
Savannah Jazz Festival
Savannah State University (WHCJ FM Radio Station)
Teeple's Seafood Restaurant
Tybee Hotel
West Broad Street YMCA

In addition to Savannah, other cities in Georgia, Florida, and neighboring South Carolina have also supported, advocated, and presented jazz. The following list reflects some of the many entities:

Georgia
    Churchill Grounds Jazz Club
    Emory University
    Georgia State University
    Kennesaw State University
    Valdosta State University
    Velvet Note Jazz Club

South Carolina
    Chef and Clef
    College of Charleston
    Forte Jazz Lounge
    Golden Rose Club/Park
    Gullah Festival
    Gullah House
    Henry's Jazz Club
    Hunter Gathering Jazz Club
    Jazz Corner (Junior Jazz Foundation)
    Jenkins Orphanage
    The Mezz
    Moja Festival
    Spoleto/Piccolo Spoleto Festival
Florida
    Douglas Anderson School of the Arts
    Florida A&M University
    Florida State University
    Jacksonville Jazz Festival
    Jacksonville University
    North East Florida Jazz Association
    University of North Florida

Real Jazz Clubs

Good Times Jazz Bar and Restaurant

Owners of Good Times Jazz Bar and Rest., Stephen and Danielle Moore

Me drummer Quinten Baxter, Chef Joe Randal, owner Stephen Moore

Good Times interior photo

Good Times Jazz Bar and Restaurant (formerly Kokopelli's Jazz Club) is the brainstorm of owners Stephen and Danielle Moore. Presently, it is the only all-jazz club of the highest level that exists in Savannah. The club has live jazz performances six times per week and a Sunday morning gospel brunch with performances ranging from local to international levels.

The club has existed in Savannah for more than sixteen years. After the closure of Kokopelli's in 2009, the building was renovated, and a new approach was developed and implemented in 2018. Upon reopening, Stephen Moore, the owner, employed Master Chef Joe Randall, as chef and consultant. Chef Joe Randall is a renowned and celebrated chef, who has distinguished himself by being one of four chefs featured in the Smithsonian's African American Museum of History and Culture.

Chef Joe Randall recommended me for the music director's position, and he and owners Stephen and Danielle Moore have relied upon my experience as a professional musician and given me their full trust regarding booking the acts. Since its reopening, Good Times has become an in-demand venue for many of the best artists in jazz, and patrons have been very supportive because of its reputation for superb food and music. The following is just a partial list of artists who have graced the bandstand at Good Times:

Nat Adderly Jr.
Eric Alexander
Rashied Ali
Scotty Barnhart
Quentin Baxter
Nicolas Bearde
Seamus Blake
Juny Booth
Carmen Bradford
Doug Carn
Emmet Cohen
Freddy Cole
Theo Croker
Delbert Felix
Sullivan Fortner
Benito Gonzalez
Wycliffe Gordon
Ellis Marsalis
Jason Marsalis
Elliott Mason
Jimmy McGriff
Tony Monaco
Johnny O'Neal
Dred "Perky" Scott
Ulysses Owens Jr.
Ike Stubblefield
Doug Wamble
Fred Wesley
Eric Wyatt

The Flamingo Night Club (Sloppy's Joint; owner, William "Sloppy" Joe Bellinger)

The Flamingo Club located on West Gwinnett Street was the hippest club for Blacks in Savannah during the fifties and sixties. Because the club never had a license to sell alcohol, events for children and adults were held there, which included high school dances, proms, as well as concerts and adult events. Legally, the club only sold setups (ice, sodas, food), and alcoholic beverages were brought to the club by adults (BYOB).

The events presented ranged from local, regional, to national acts. The genres of entertainment and music included blues, rhythm and blues, jazz, and floor shows. I was fortunate to be a regular performer throughout my high school years until I joined the US Air Force and left Savannah. The Flamingo brought the biggest names in entertainment. I remember seeing Ray Charles, Buddy Johnson, Bill Doggett, B. B. King, Bobby Bland, Duke Ellington, Count Basie, and many other iconic acts.

Sunday night shows emulated New York clubs or the likes thereof. As a member of the house band the Blue Notes, led by drummer Val Davis (profiled in *The Up of the Down Beat*), the club presented a jazz concert and floor show that could have been held in any major city that offered professional and enjoyable entertainment. The club was packed every Sunday night, and because it did not legally sell alcohol, children were allowed. Of course, alcohol could be purchased under the table.

A typical Sunday night show would include a jazz concert of well-rehearsed tunes by the Blue Notes, comedians, vocalists, tap dancers, and singing groups. The acts were rehearsed on Saturdays and usually rendered polished performances on Sunday nights. Savannah had several outstanding performers living in the city, and other sojourners and guests would come to town because of the Sunday night sets. The audiences were comprised of people from all walks of life, ranging from regular working-class people to Savannah's professional and quasi-bourgeois residents.

I can still vividly recall dancers like Twinkle Toe Singleton, vocalists Stella Storms and Moon Lawton, and several singing groups that had not only perfected their vocals but also performed great precision choreography. Sunday nights at the Flamingo were appreciated and well supported. The nostalgia still reminds me of how fortunate I was to witness and be a part of it.

Hannah's (Hard Hearted Hannah's, Hannah's East)

Owner and bass player extraordinaire Ben Tucker

Hannah's was the jazz heartbeat of Savannah for more than twelve years (mid-eighties to mid-nineties). The owner and renowned bass player Ben Tucker never compromised the music and occasionally brought national acts in. When national acts were not performing, Ben always showcased outstanding musicians. He maintained a very strong trio that served as the house band. Some of the better piano players who played in Savannah were a result of being a part of Ben's trios, i.e., Joe "Virginia" Jones, Kevin Bales, Doug Carn, Tommy Gill, Kenny Palmer, and John Colianni, just naming a few. Also drummers included Von Barlow, Eric Vaughn, Samarai Celestial, Val Davis, Ron Free, Teddy Lender, and many more.

Hannah's was a very popular tourist spot as well as a local favorite. It was an ideal location for many movie scenes. Emma Kelly, "The Lady of 1,000 songs" was also a nightly feature and an in-demand attraction. Hannah's truly represented and perpetuated Savannah's legacy as being an important contributor to the art of jazz.

Rancho Alegre Cuban Restaurant

Jodi Espina, Maggie and Jackson Evans,
regular performers at Ranch Alegre

Interior of Rancho Alegre

Rancho Alegre is an authentic Cuban restaurant owned and operated by restaurateur and jazz advocate Juan Rodriguez. It has become one of Savannah's most popular places for both great food and live jazz. Opening in 1999 on Posey Street, Southside Savannah, Rancho Alegre quickly gained a reputation for its ambience and delicious Cuban cuisine.

Outgrowing its limited space on Posey Street, Juan relocated the restaurant to Martin Luther King Blvd in 2010 and quickly established it as not only an in-demand dining location but also an ideal room for enjoying great jazz music. Spearheading the jazz presence at Rancho Alegre is saxophonist/entrepreneur, Jody Espina, who has been responsible for its perpetuation since the relocation more than fourteen years now. Rancho Alegre is responsible for being part of the revitalization of jazz in Savannah. It has hosted several jazz events and offers regular work for jazz musicians in Savannah.

The Jazz Corner

Owners Bob and Lois Masteller

Interior of The Jazz Corner

The Jazz Corner is located on Hilton Head Island and has been recognized as being one of the Top 100 Great Jazz Rooms in the world by *DownBeat* magazine. Celebrating over twenty years of presenting sensational entertainment paired with gourmet cuisine, the club is a culmination of what the late jazz musician and historian Bob Masteller set out to accomplish for jazz lovers. Confidently managed by Kelli Lesch and Lois Masteller, the club's menu, superbly managed by Chef Wade, offers Southern cuisine that compares to the same level of jazz that is presented nightly. Over the last twenty-four years, many renowned artists have appeared at the Jazz Corner:

Bob Alberti
Monty Alexander
Mose Allison
Emmet Cohen
Freddy Cole
Noel Freidline
Champion Fulton
Wycliffe Gordon
Maria Howell
Rene Marie
Ellis Marsalis

Kate McGarry
Deana Martin
Bucky Pizzarelli
Lynn Roberts
Bria Skonberg
Marlena Smalls
Ben Tucker

Adagio Jazz Club

Owner Salah Abdul-Wahid

Owner, organist Doug Carn

The Adagio Jazz Club, although short-lived, deserves inclusion in the list of jazz ventures in Savannah, Georgia. From 2002 until 2006, Adagio, the brainstorm of jazz organist Doug Carn and entrepreneur Salah Abdul-Wahid, was a breath of fresh air in Savannah. The club maintained an ideal ambience and featured an array of impressive musicians:

Carl Allen
Doug Carn
Judy Bady
Laïka Fatien (France)
Giacomo Gates
Rufus Harley (bagpipes)
Antonio Hart
Dr Eddie Henderson
Obie Jesse
Kent Jordan
Stephanie Jordan
Frank Lacey
Ellis Marsalis
Danny Mixon
Bill Saxon
Ben Tucker
Steve Williams

The club was able to present superb solo acts because of Doug Carn's connections in the jazz world and his able and ready accompaniment on either piano or the Hammond B3 organ. The club was also a shot in the arm for both local and regional artists. Adagio allowed me to assemble several impressive bands for performances there and, when I was not gigging regularly, offered an outlet for me to play and keep my chops in shape. In my opinion, Adagio was an important part of Savannah's history and jazz legacy.

The Mezz

Me and music director for the Mezz, two times
grammy winner and drummer, Quentin Baxter

The Mezz Bar was a force to be reckoned with. From August of
2012 to early 2015, music director and drummer/composer Quentin
Baxter graced its bandstand with perpetual outstanding jazz acts.
Located on the second floor of Sermet's Mediterranean Restaurant,
The Mezz showcased an outstanding quintet nightly led by Baxter.
The music was fresh and up to date. The quintet that included Mark
Sterbank on woodwinds, Charlton Singleton on trumpet/flugelhorn,
Richard White Jr. on piano, and Kevin Hamilton on bass superbly
represented what the essence of jazz should be.

In addition to an outstanding house band and great food, the
club featured the following very impressive national artists:

Mitch Butler
Etienne Charles
Freddy Cole Quartet
Keith Davis Trio
Wycliffe Gordon
Rene Marie

Tony Monaco Trio
Marcus Roberts Trio
Audrey Shakir

The Mezz was also a welcomed outlet for local and regional musicians. It was an important part of Charleston's jazz history and legacy. Thanks, Quentin Baxter, for all you have done and what you are still doing for the CAUSE.

The Jenkins Orphanage

From a building that was little more than a shed located at 600 King Street with four or five children in 1891 to an old vacated marine hospital at 20 Franklin Street, Baptist minister Reverend Daniel Jenkins pursued and realized a dream that culminated in an orphanage that housed more than five hundred orphans and was mainly supported by its band of young aspiring musicians.

Reverend Jenkins brought in local learned musicians to teach selected orphans how to play instruments and read music who in turn would teach other children over the years. The band eventually developed a Southern syncopated jazz style similar to that of New Orleans but with a Gullah/Geechee influence and not only toured the nation but also performed abroad. Known for strong brass instruments as well as other instruments, the orphanage produced some of the best and influential jazz players in the history of the music who included Sylvester Briscoe, Jabbo Smith, Cat Anderson, Freddie Green, Speedy Jones, Peanuts Holland, and Geechee Fields to name a few.

Jenkins Orphanage musicians made their mark in jazz by playing with many jazz icons who included Fletcher Henderson, Bennie Moten, Jelly Roll Morton, Duke Ellington, and Count Basie, and the list does not end there. Many children who were not orphans became members of the Jenkins Orphanage band because of its success and reputation. Although not known for music, the Jenkins Orphanage, presently known as the Jenkins Institute for Children, is still in existence and thriving.

Spoleto Festival

For almost fifty years, Charleston, South Carolina, has presented the Spoleto Festival to the world. Founded in 1977 by Pulitzer-winning composer Gian Carlo Menotti, Christopher Keene, and others, the goal was to create an American counterpart to the world-renowned Spoleto Festival in Italy. This festival is quite eclectic, covering several genres of music with an impressive focus on jazz. This writer has been privileged to catch live performances by some of the greatest jazz artists who ever embraced the art form. It would be most difficult to attempt a listing of past acts.

Picolo Spoleto, a part of the festival that focuses on regional and local acts, is also an important aspect and combines its acts with the national/international performances to make the Spoleto Festival a worthwhile experience for everyone to have.

The Chef & Clef

The Chef & Clef was an important and impactful jazz entity in Charleston, South Carolina, for more than ten years. Owner and drummer Charlie Gahn featured some outstanding performers during that period. The club, located on Market Street, consisted of three levels, the second being an extension of the first and the third floor featuring different genres of music other than jazz.

The club offered local, regional, and national artists a place to perform. I recall being paired or featured with quite a few different musicians who were of the highest caliber whenever I played there. The Chef & Clef was a popular venue during Spoleto and Piccolo festivals. It was known for hosting great jam sessions that included both local and national artists, including Branford Marsalis, Horace Silver, Lionel Hampton, Dave Brubeck, and Maynard Ferguson to name a few, who graced the bandstand at the club because of its popularity, location, and reputation. The Chef & Clef was an important part of Charleston's jazz legacy.

The Velvet Note (The Acoustic Living Room)

Owner of The Velvet Note Tamara Fuller

Interior of The Velvet Note

The Velvet Note is presently one of the better clubs in the Atlanta area that is dedicated to the essence of the art form commonly referred to as jazz. Very ably managed by owner/chef Tamara

Fuller, this establishment has presented the following impressive lineup of who's who in jazz:

Larry Carlton
Dennis Chambers
Cyrus Chestnut
Jimmy Cobb
Freddy Cole
Kenny Garrett
Robert Glasper
Julian Lage
Ronnie Laws
Jazzmen Horn
Delfeayo Marsalis
Pat Martino
Christian McBride
Gretchen Parlato
Marcus Roberts
Wallace Roney
Christian Sands
Diane Schuur
Mike Stern
Bobby Watson
Jeff "Tain" Watts
Dave Weckl

Also known as the Acoustic Living Room, the club's ambience speaks for itself (seats about sixty people and has a warm, homey atmosphere). When I inquired why Alpharetta instead of downtown Atlanta, Tamara stated her research had revealed that a decline for support of the arts and inconsistency of regular patronage for the arts were important factors. Other factors that helped decide on Alpharetta were the high rate of employment, a hunger in the area for entertainment, and the close proximity of educational institutions that have a jazz presence.

The musicians who I personally know speak very highly of both the club's ambience and cuisine. I'm sure that the city of Alpharetta and jazz lovers from Atlanta are grateful and appreciative of Tamara Fuller's affinity for jazz and her effort and dedication to maintaining a great club that represents, in my opinion, America's highest music art form. Kudos, Tamara. Keep doin' what you're doin'.

Churchill Grounds Jazz Bar

For almost twenty years, Churchill Grounds Jazz Bar/Café was Atlanta's premier jazz spot. Located in downtown Atlanta on Peachtree Street near the famous Fox Theater, this venue served as a showcase for local, regional, national, and international performers. Owner Sam Yi can be given credit for maintaining an incredible posture for several years. Not only was Churchill Grounds the most prominent venue for the best jazz performances, but it established a high standard for outstanding jam sessions.

A list of artists who performed there would be too expensive. The ambience and location combined equaled or in some cases surpassed jazz venues located in other major cities. Its tenured presence in Atlanta was greatly responsible for a very vibrant jazz music scene being there, and because of its popularity, Atlanta gained the temporary and permanent relocation of fantastic musicians from everywhere. Although Churchill Grounds closed in 2017, its impact is still being realized by the city.

The Savanah Music Festival

Executive Director of The Savannah Music Festival, Gene Dobbs Bradford

The Savannah Music Festival has been in existence for thirty-five-plus years and is considered to be one of the top music events in existence. Each year, the festival exposes Savannah and tourists from all fifty states and abroad to an eclectic presentation of performances that include jazz, classical, American, and international roots music. This festival has grown and expanded tremendously throughout the years.

Presently under the executive directorship of Gene Dobbs Bradford, who has a wealth of knowledge and experience that also includes a degree in classical bass violin performance from the Eastman School of Music, one of the finest schools in the country, the Savannah Music Festival is soaring to even greater heights than ever.

Space does not permit a listing of the varied artistic performances that have been presented over the years. Prior to the beginning of this festival, I thought that Charleston, South Carolina's, Spoleto Festival was impressive, but in my opinion, the Savannah Music Festival has eclipsed Spoleto and is equal to or better than any other festival of its kind anywhere. I cannot think of any jazz act or musician of note that has not been featured at its performances.

In addition to the festival's outstanding performances, its education outreach, SMF Jazz Academy (SMFJA), is both motivational and rewarding. The program offers free one-on-one lessons to students in grades fifth through twelfth. Instruments, materials, and meals are included in this after-school program and are also free. Students are exposed to jazz at an early age by a faculty of eight qualified instructors. What an ideal approach to perpetuating and exposing our youth to this great indigenous art form called jazz. At the helm of the faculty is Benge Daneman. He is an acclaimed trumpet player and doing a fantastic job.

Owner Jodi Espina with the Count Basie Orchestra.
Saxophone section plays Jodi Jazz mouthpieces.

In addition to musicians, venues, special events, festivals, and schools, there are also entities that are important and have influence on the jazz culture in this area. In Savannah, we have two such entities, Jody Jazz Saxophone Mouthpiece Manufactory and Benedetto Guitar Company.

Jody Espina, professional saxophonist/clarinetist, educator, and recording artist, is the founder and owner of Jody Jazz. Jody is reputed to manufacture one of the world's finest saxophone mouthpieces. Some of the most renowned saxophonists, who include Tom Scott, Don Braden, Jeff Loffin, and the Count Basie Orchestra Saxophone Section, are all endorsees of Jody Jazz mouthpieces. Jody Jazz has been located in Savannah since 2008. The factory uses modern equipment, employs experienced technicians, and guarantees both quality productions and improved/updated mouthpieces. There is always something new and enhanced available for discerning saxophone players.

Along with Jody Jazz, Howard Paul, guitarist extraordinaire, has helped perpetuate Benedetto Guitars as one of the most in-demand guitars in the jazz arena. He became president of the company when Bob Benedetto opened his factory in Savannah in 2006. Upon Bob's retirement, Vintner (Napa Valley), Dave Miner became its principal investor. Howard continues to maintain the reputation and stability of the business.

The company has about a dozen employees, and under the expertise of maerlutheir Damon Mailand, Benedetto has a projected goal of one hundred guitars per year. In addition to being at the helm of Benedetto Guitars, Howard is a standout in the Savannah community and is developing quite a national reputation as a frequently requested guitarist.

The Savannah Jazz Festival

Ben Tucker and Teddy Adams, among headliners

Typical weekend daytime attendance at the
first Savannah Jazz Festival, 1983

Typical weekend night attendance at the Savannah Jazz Festival

Now in its forty-second year and forty-third festival, the Savannah Jazz Festival ("Bands and Organizations," *The Up of the Down Beat*) is still one of the best music events in Savannah. Even the COVID-19 pandemic did not cause its cancellation. The festival streamed on television and was seen by millions all over the world.

The Savannah Jazz Festival attracts thousands of citizens and visitors and tremendously boosts Savannah's economy. Savannah Jazz, the City of Savannah, and numerous businesses and sponsors are consistent with their efforts to perpetuate this event. People from a varied social stratification inundate all of the week-long events, and in forty-three years, there has never been a negative outburst or disorder at any of the events/venues. Although various venues throughout the city are used, Forsyth Park, Savannah's largest outdoor location, is still the festival's mainstay.

The Savannah Jazz Festival is still free and open to the general public. Over the past years, the festival has presented some of jazz's most noted icons. The following is only a partial listing of artists and performers who have been a part of this monumental event:

Art Blakey and the Jazz Messengers
Kenny Barron
Ray Charles
Ravi Coltrane
Joey DeFrancesco
Jon Faddis
Curtis Fuller
Benny Golson
Lionel Hampton
Jimmy and Tootie Heath
Jon Hendrix
Ahmad Jamal
Ramsey Lewis
Herbie Mann
Christian McBride
Carmen McCrae
Mulgrew Miller
Nicolas Payton
Ben Riley
Jimmy Smith
Sphere
Clark Terry
McCoy Tyner
Joe Williams
Nancy Wilson

Savannah Jazz Festival Photo Gallery

The following photo gallery reflects a few of the jazz artists who have performed at the Savannah Jazz Festival over the past forty-three years (1983 to Present). All festivals are free and open to the general public.

The Savannah Jazz Orchestra

Bassist Rufus Reid

Giacomo Gates

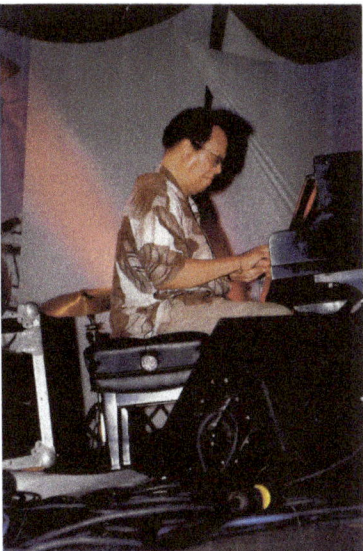

Cedar Walton

Fred Wesley

Dianne Shuur

Herman Riley and Teddy Adams

Mark Whitfield

Roy Ayers

Cindy Blackman

Steve Nelson

Ravi Coltrane

David "Fat Head" Newman

Mulgrew Miller

Ben Riley, Mulgrew Miller, Teddy Adams, Buster Williams

Benny Golson and Teddy Adams

Lenny White

Joanne Brackeen

Rashied Ali

Jon Hendrix

Albert "Tootie" Heath

James "Blood" Ulmer

James Moody

Sonny Fortune

"Bunky" Green

Quentin Baxter

Frank Morgan

Javon Jackson

Irene Reid

Betty "Bebop" Carter

Jimmy Heath

Marlena Shaw

Joey Defrancesco, "Buby McMillian, Teddy Adams

Eric Wyatt, Teddy Adams, Jeff
"Tain" Watts, Marius Van Den Brink

Marcus Printup
(trumpet Player)

Kevin Mahogany (vocalist)

Don Braden and Valery Ponomarev

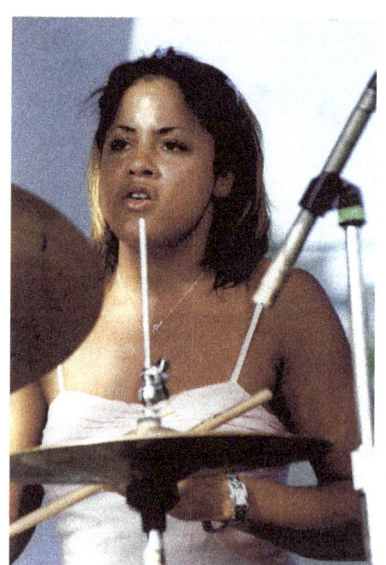

Kim Thompson

Jane Bunnett

Eddie Gomez

Odean Pope

Ingrid Jensen

Carmen Bradford

Vanessa Rubin

Rodney Jordan

Wayne Escoffery

Vincent Gardener

Left to right - Teddy Adams, George Harper, and Charles Tolliver

Left to right - Carl Allen, Christian McBride, and Ike Carter

Fred Wesley and Curtis Fuller

Rufus Reid and Gary Bartz

Eddie Pazant

Esperanza Spalding and Teddy Adams

Donald Byrd

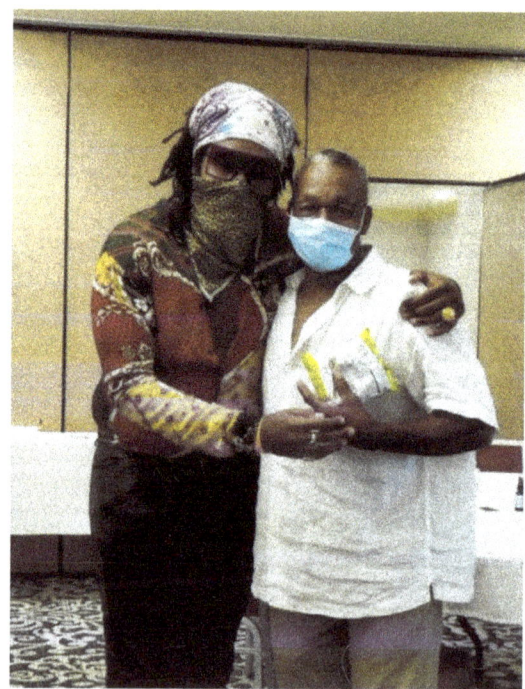

Russell Hall and Delbert Felix

The Annual Christmas Concert and Jam Session

Ben Tucker and Teddy Adams promotion for the
Annual Christmas Concert and Jam Session

To date, the Annual Christmas Concert and Jam Session is the
longest-running jazz event in Savannah. Beginning in the mid-fif-
ties as a fundraiser for the all black AFM (American Federation of
Musicians local 704), it was held every Christmas Day until the
mid-sixties before being discontinued. Upon my return to Savannah
after a sixteen-year absence, I was astonished to find that the musicians were still here but jazz had dissipated. One of my first endeav-
ors was to reestablish this event.

Along with my brother, Bobby, vocalists Stella Storms and
Lafayette Chester, and drummer Bobby Vaughn, we started holding
the concerts every year at different locations as fundraisers for various worthwhile organizations. The popularity was rekindled, and the
event soon became a lure for both musicians and residents who had
moved away and returned home for Christmas.

Presently, the Annual Christmas Concert and Jam Session has
been in existence for more than fifty years and is one of the main
jazz events of the year. For the past several years, it has been held as
a major fundraiser for Savannah Jazz, drawing hundreds of patrons
and necessitating larger venues.

Savannah Jazz

Executive Director Savannah Jazz, Paula Fogarty

Ribbon cutting and dedication ceremonies for the Jazz
History and Hall of Fame Exhibit, left to right
Mayor of Savannah Van Johnson, Paula Fogarty, Teddy Adams
(cutting the ribbon), Savannah Jazz President Colin Schofield

Savannah Jazz (formerly The Coastal Jazz Association; "Bands and Organizations," *The Up of the Down Beat*) has been in existence since 1982 and presently has more than a thousand members. It is a nonprofit organization, and its main goal is to advocate, support, educate, and perpetuate the great art form called jazz and keep Savannah's history and legacy alive.

A board of directors, president, and executive director are responsible for maintaining and executing the many demands that are necessary for its successful operation. Along with various committees and dedicated members, Savannah Jazz consistently does everything possible to preserve this American indigenous art form. The organization's latest historically significant achievement is the successful completion and opening of the Savannah Jazz History and Hall of Fame Exhibit.

After three years of fundraising and planning, the Savannah Jazz History and Hall of Fame Exhibit is open in the Savannah History Museum. Raising over $140,000 for the project not including in-kind donations, the organization is bringing Savannah's rich jazz history to life.

Executive Director of Savannah Jazz, Paula Fogarty, says:

> Our City's jazz history is as old and significant as that of New Orleans, but the story has yet to be told. This exhibit will not only be a legacy project for our organization, but for the City of Savannah itself. It will serve as the keystone for our educational programs enlightening newcomers to jazz and aficionados about this history. We are thrilled to collaborate with the Coastal Heritage Society and the Savannah History Museum.

The world-class exhibit design firm Riggs-Ward was engaged to help create the exhibit; they were selected based on their excellent work for the Library of Congress, New Orleans Jazz Museum, Black History Museum and Cultural Center, and the Smithsonian.

The content was developed in consultation with jazz historian Dr. Charles Elmore and with Teddy Adams and Dr. Otis Johnson.

Like New Orleans, Savannah was one of jazz's birthplaces and has been a leading center of the art form through its noted composers, performers, venues, festivals, media, and businesses since the 1920s. Deeply rooted in African traditions, Savannah jazz has evolved through brass bands, vaudeville, blues, big band, combos, and orchestras to take its place in our nation's jazz pantheon. Following its near demise in 1960 resulting from the ascendency of rhythm and blues and rock 'n' roll, Savannah jazz was reborn in the late 1970s through the efforts of Teddy Adams and the legendary Ben Tucker. The Coastal Jazz Association, now known as Savannah Jazz, was founded in 1982 and today continues to be the custodian of Savannah's jazz legacy with our Annual Savannah Jazz Festival, monthly concerts, The Ben Tucker Memorial Concert, and educational programs.

Utilizing a combination of artifacts, displays, and interactive multimedia, the exhibit will illustrate Savannah's storied jazz history from its inception to today. A key component is the Savannah Jazz Hall of Fame, now totaling forty-five inductees who represent the who's who in the jazz world. Biographies, visuals about their lives, and their music and contributions to jazz will clearly establish Savannah's place as a major center for the art form. From Joe "King" Oliver, Louis Armstrong's mentor, to Johnny Mercer, Savannah's famed composer and vocalist, to acclaimed bassist and composer Ben Tucker, who led the jazz revival from the seventies, the Jazz Hall of Fame will give visitors an understanding of the legends of Savannah jazz.

The evolution of jazz in Savannah, from its earliest incarnations to the present, will be the main focus of the exhibit. Visuals and stores of the vibrant old West Broad Street (now MLK Blvd.) scene will illustrate the importance of this once-great jazz mecca. Images of Tybrisa Pavilion, the legendary dance hall on Tybee Island that hosted the top big bands of the day, black and white, will bring this big band scene to life. Artifacts on display will include Ben Tucker's historic bass violin, Johnny Mercer's Oscar award for *Moon River*, and other memorabilia; artifacts from the estate of James Moody including his favorite horn, photos, and posters from Savannah Jazz Festival and acclaimed concerts with the top jazz performers in the world; and recordings and videos of legends who performed in Savannah (Article from 2022 Savannah Jazz Festival, "Updated Savannah Jazz Hall of Fame).

Ben Tucker, Kenny Palmer, Teddy Adams,
among first hall of fame inductees

*The Savannah Jazz Hall of F*ame. Since its establishment, the Hall of Fame has inducted several members. The following reflect the prerequisites for inclusion:

1. Nominees must have been born in Savannah or in the immediate area or have lived in Savannah or the immediate area for at least fifteen years.
2. Nominees must have distinguished themselves as musicians, educators, historians, or writers on a national or international level.
3. Nominees who meet the necessary criteria, excluding being born or living in Savannah for at least fifteen years, must have an important aspect of their lives significantly associated with Savannah.

4. Nominees who have not achieved national status as jazz performers, educators, historians, or writers must have distinguished themselves through outstanding support, promotion, or other contributions to the perpetuation of the jazz art form.

Savannah Jazz Hall of Fame inductees:

Teddy Adams, trombone
Nat Allen, trombone
Quentin Baxter, drums
Lee Blair, guitar
Benjamin G. Brown, trumpet, educator
Lucious Bryant Jr., drums
Theron "Ike" Carter, advocate
Samarai Celestial (Eric Walker), drums
Charlie Chisholm, trumpet
Varnell "Val" Davis, drums
Frank Dilworth, promoter
Bob Faircloth, advocate, philanthropist
Charles Elmore, author, advocate
Jody Espina, saxophone
Delbert Felix, bass
Sam Gill, trumpet
Tom Glaser, advocate
Bobby Greene, saxophone
Connie Haines, vocalist
George Harper, saxophone
Julias "Boo" Hornstein, advocate, author
Richard "Skip" Jennings, advocate
Otis Johnson, advocate
Joe Jones, piano
Eric Jones, piano
Kahn Keene, trombone
Herbert King, drums
Kirk Lee, trumpet

Kaiser Marshall, drums
Robert "Bob" Masteller, trumpet, trombone, vibraphone
Johnny Mercer, composer
Theodore "Stubby" Mitchell, trumpet
James Moody, saxophone
Joseph "King" Oliver, trumpet
Kenny Palmer, piano
Howard Paul, guitar
Eddie Pazant, saxophone
Randall Reese, saxophone
Daniel Ray (aka Big Black), percussion
Irene Reid, vocalist
Ben Riley, drums
Huxsie Scott, vocalist
Sahib Shihab (Edmond Gregory), saxophone
Cladys "Jabbo" Smith, trumpet
Joe Steele, piano
Eric Vaughn, drums
James Osborne "Trummy" Young, trombone

Hangin' with the "Cats"

Me, Earl, and Kebbi (Earl, deceased, and Kebbi Williams, very much alive)

Earl and Kebbi are father-and-son saxophonists. Both are very talented but chose different musical paths. Earl, from Tennessee State University, and Kebbi, Howard University, are both very interesting musicians. Earl began his career as a very serious jazz player on saxophones and bass but later decided that he preferred entertaining more than playing, so comedy and a harmonica were added to his act, and he became known and appreciated more as an entertainer than a serious jazz musician. He loved what he was doing and was quite good at it. His audiences certainly supported and enjoyed him. To say the least, he worked all the time.

Contrary to his father, Kebbi is about as serious as anyone can be about the pure creative approach to playing jazz. Although he has an affinity for avant-garde jazz, he is more than capable of playing straight-ahead jazz. As a matter of fact, he is one of my favorite saxophone players and has played and recorded with me.

Both of them are very hip dudes and a lot of fun to hang with. I have played with Kebbi more often than his dad because we are more musically in tune. Although they chose different musical paths, like father, like son, the talent is there. I can vividly recall Kebbi's moving tribute to Earl at his funeral. Before Kebbi performed, a video of Earl playing a beautiful and moving soprano solo of "The Lord's Prayer" was shown. Kebbi then entered from the rear of the church playing his father's soprano saxophone (he had never played soprano before) and delivered one of the hippest renditions of "Amazing Grace" that I have ever heard. True to his ability to play both in and out musically, he still captured the essence, spirit, and meaning of the song. Of course, he brought the congregation to their feet showing uncontrollable emotions and appreciation.

Me and Kevin (Kevin Bales)

Another fine pianist from Atlanta is Kevin Bales. I have known him since he was attending the University of North Florida. He was playing regularly with bassist Ben Tucker on weekends at Hannah's Jazz Club, which Ben owned. I could immediately tell that Kevin was going to become a fine piano player, and he certainly did. We have been playing together for a number of years, and his growth is astonishing. He has also recorded with me. What I like most about Kevin is his attitude about playing the music. He respects and enjoys it and has always given me respect for what I am attempting to do for the art form commonly referred to as jazz. What stands out the most to me about Kevin is his unchanging response when I call him for a gig. Sometimes, the money isn't that great, or there might not be an accompanying room, which is a serious consideration when you have to travel almost three hundred miles to play, but here is the answer that I always get, "Teddy, man, if I'm not working, the money is not important. I like playing, and I enjoy playing with or for you." That says a lot to me.

Me and Eric (Eric Jones)

Eric Jones, a Savannahian by way of Moultrie, Georgia, has lived here more than twenty years. He is a graduate of Armstrong and Georgia Southern Universities. Eric is a fine pianist, composer, and arranger, who, although a jazz pianist, has an affinity for both classical and church music. That equates to being well-rounded. I have seen incredible growth and dedication to this music called jazz. I work with him regularly because I recommended him for the house gig at Good Times Jazz Bar and Restaurant, where I play and serve as musical director. Eric has a positive attitude about life and the music. Presently, Eric has perhaps the best small group, Eric Jones Trio, in this area. He is ably accompanied by two extraordinary musicians in the persons of Marc Chesanow on bass and Robert Saunders on drums. Marc is an Eastman Music School graduate, who is equally adept playing jazz or classical music, and Robert is a drummer extraordinaire, who displays incredible skills and creativity. I expect great accomplishments from both him and his trio. Hey, man, don't change. Keep doin' what you're doin'.

Me and Lawrence (Lawrence "Hutch" Hutchins Jr.)

If you're lucky, you have a few people that you can regard as friends during your life. Of course, there are good acquaintances, but friends are rare. Most of my friends are no longer on the planet, but I still have a few, about three to be exact. One of them is Lawrence.

I have known him since the first grade at East Broad Street Elementary School. We were casual friends and did not become fully aware of one another until 1952 in the fifth grade when the public school band program implemented for black students (the program for white kids began in 1948). By the time we started high school, we had become the best of friends.

Lawrence and I have a lot in common. Perhaps that's why we have remained friends for so long. Although he never pursued being a jazz woodwindist, his understanding of music theory and the profoundness of jazz has allowed him to be a strong supporter and advocate. We differ in many ways with choices of habits, but an observer would never detect it. Our friendship and mutual respect for each other transcend our differences. Our commonalities are strong, and the bond between us is solid.

Hanging with him is the same as being with fellow jazz musicians. He understands and has an affinity for jazz that equals mine, thereby creating an air of comfort and enjoyment when we are together, and that's quite frequently.

Me and Eric (Eric Wyatt, saxophonist)

Eric Wyatt Quintet at Good Times Jazz Bar And Rest.,
from left to right Eric Wyatt, Xavier Breaker,
Delbert Felix, Teddy Adams, Eric Jones

I would be remiss if I did not include this segment in my book. Saxophonist extraordinaire Eric Wyatt is a gifted musician, and there is a very obvious reason for that. He is the son of a saxophonist, Charles Wyatt, and the godson of one of the three greatest saxophonists who ever graced this planet. In my humble opinion, Charlie Parker, Sonny Rollins, and John Coltrane epitomize the jazz saxophone. Eric's godfather is none other than the Colossal One, Sonny Rollins.

Eric is presently playing Sonny's horn that he gave to Eric's father. I had the pleasure of playing with Eric at Good Times Jazz Bar and Restaurant. It was the most enjoyable gig, playing and listening. The rhythm section included Delbert Felix, Eric Jones, and Xavier Breaker, great trio.

Presently, Eric and his sister, Carol, are two of the few people who are in contact with Sonny on a regular basis. Eric has known Sonny most of his cognizant life. He informed me of some very interesting trivia about Sonny. For instance, when Sonny first met Charlie Parker, Bird's comment was, "You sound just like me." Mind you, Sonny was still a teenager. According to Eric, Sonny was not surprised because he knew he had shredded (practiced) and deduced himself to studying Bird, the pioneer of modern improvisation.

Eric also told me that Sonny knows what he wants musically and will not settle for anything less. He said that Sonny is particular about his drummers partially because of what he wanted when he played calypso music. Being of Caribbean descent, he loves calypso rhythm and has written several calypso tunes besides "St. Thomas." I then asked why Bob Crenshaw always played electric bass instead of acoustic, and the answer was similar: it was more conducive to play calypso music.

Eric also told me that he goes out of his way to stay in touch with Sonny because he is in somewhat of a depressed state. Having lost his wife, not being able to play his horn because of physical reasons, and confronted with the loss of his close friends and peers have taken somewhat of a toll on him.

It was nice hanging and playing with Eric because Sonny Rollins has always been one of my favorite musicians, even before I became aware of John Coltrane. It was very enlightening, rewarding, and uplifting to find out that someone who knows Sonny so well and is dedicated to perpetuating his music and improvisational contribution to jazz is doing it with both dedication and musical authority. Keep doin' what you doin', Eric.

Me and Robert (Robert Saunders, promising drummer with unlimited potential)

Robert is my first call drummer in Savannah, although hard to nail down sometimes. He's cooperative and versatile and has a memory like an elephant. When I use him in my sextet, giving the music to him is a mere formality. He knows and remembers the arrangements very well. Starting as a church drummer and later gravitating to other genres of music, he has proven to be adept and comfortable wherever he's needed.

Love, a baby, and marriage have interrupted his formal training, but I understand familial commitment. I'm sure he is getting tired of me reminding him of the need for an educational/formal background in music, but it doesn't stop me from doing it. That's the way it's done now. He has the innate qualities, but joining the competition on an equal level is a kind of insurance. He might as well get used to me bugging him because that's exactly what I'm going to continue to do.

Me and Louis Heriveaux

Appearing a Good Times Jazz Bar and Rest., Nic Beard, Louis Heriveaux, Teddy Adams

I first heard Louis when he was still in high school. I formally met him two years later through one of my former mentees, drummer Eric Vaughn. Louis has always been an impressive pianist. I remember when I first heard him play at a jam session. He was the only student who sat in, and the adults, who were all band directors and professional musicians, let him play toward the end of the session. To my pleasant surprise, he sounded as good or better than the other piano players who were there. I have watched and listened to Louis over the years and witnessed his incredible growth and development. Presently, I consider him to be one of the best piano players that I have had the pleasure of listening to and/or playing with.

When I hear him play, I don't compare him to his peers. I compare him to the consummate cats who are on a national level. Not only is he an outstanding player but also a very humble individual who is a pleasure to work with. Although the recognition process is slow, Louis's name is being circulated in the right circles. It's just a matter of time before he receives his just due.

Those who are not aware of who Louis Heriveaux is are in for a pleasant surprise in the very near future. Inevitably and destiny are synonymous and won't be denied. Keep doin' what you're doin', lil' brother.

Me and Rufus (Rufus Reid, Rufus-San)

Rufus Reid was the first guy that I met in Japan. Both he and I were in the United States Air Force. We became instant friends. I had just left Washington, DC, and really did not want to be in Japan. The Washington music scene was very hip, and I was quite satisfied living there. I was hanging and playing with the best musicians, including Bobby Timmons, Wilbur Ware, Jimmy Hopps, Eddie Henderson, and Nathan Page to name a few. I was somewhat depressed and did not attempt to embrace Tokyo. It was Rufus who informed me that the Japanese were serious and appreciative of jazz. He finally persuaded me to go to Tokyo with him, and I got the surprise of my life when I heard the Cats play.

Rufus had been living in Tokyo for about two or three years before I got there and knew how to move around the city very well. He introduced me to several musicians, and I gradually began to adapt to being there and put Washington behind me. We hung out and played together all the time. He had introduced me to his friend Lee McLoy, who was also in the Air Force and a very good drummer. The three of us played and hung out together all the time.

I vividly remember walking into the band room one day, and Rufus was playing trumpet. Jokingly, I said something like, "You need to stick to playing bass." He laughed and told me that he was originally assigned to the band as a trumpet player but decided he liked the bass better and did not begin playing bass until he had been in the air force for a while. He could see the look of disbelief on my face. He was obviously a natural and not interested in the trumpet anymore. After about a year, Rufus returned to the United States and began taking private lessons.

He and I corresponded regularly for a while. He kept me abreast of what was happening on the jazz scene in America. I remember him telling me how much he appreciated his brother's interest and support. He was living with him upon returning home. He said that his brother furnished three hots and a cot (food and a place to live). All he did was practice and take private lessons. He was accepted to Northwestern University in Chicago where he obtained his degree, and the rest is history. Rufus is now considered one of the best bass players in jazz and stays busy playing and recording with the very best musicians. I did not see him again for about six years. He came to Tokyo, playing with Nancy Wilson and Freddie Hubbard. My wife and I invited him and Doris, his wife, to dinner, and we reminisced about old times. It was beautiful, and my wife is a superb cook.

Me and Steve Turre

Me and trombonist Steve Turre

While visiting my daughter in New York, she treated me to an evening at the Blue Note. The Azar Lawrence Quintet featuring Steve Turre was performing. We got there early, and I had a chance to talk to Steve before the gig started. It was my first time meeting and hearing him in person.

It was a very hip conversation because we both had trombonist Andrae Murchison as a student. After discussing and agreeing that Andrae was developing into a fine trombone player, we briefly spoke of other trombone players. I quickly realized that Steve was a keen observer of trombone players and quite critical of those who did not speak the jazz language when playing chord changes. As well as Steve plays chord changes, he's certainly worthy of critiquing them. On the other hand, he was also quite complimentary too.

I remember him saying that Ron Westray was a great lead trombone player and Wycliffe Gordon was one of the best plunger players he had ever heard. I was really surprised at that statement because he is no slouch playing with the plunger himself. I then surprised him with the fact that Wycliffe Gordon, Ron Westray, Michael Deas, Stan Wilkerson, and Chris Crenshaw lived in the vicinity of Savannah. Even Ron Westray who is from Columbia, South Carolina, is only a little over one hundred miles away. That's quite a coincidence.

It was an interesting conversation, and I ended it by telling him how much I envied him because although he had played with most of the great players of his time, he had the good fortune of playing with two outstanding giants in the persons of Woody Shaw and Rahsaan Roland Kirk. It doesn't get any better than that, two unequalled experiences.

Me and Magic Marc (Magic Marc Dunston, magician)

My main man and favorite magician, jazz advocate, and sometimes enforcer Magic Marc is a loyal jazz advocate, producer, and supporter. Marc has been involved with Savannah Jazz (formerly Coastal Jazz Association) for several years. Whether serving as announcer, master of ceremonies, or enforcer at our jam sessions, he can be counted on to get things done. Sometimes, when things get out of hand at the jam sessions and incompetent musicians become a musical infringement, Marc is our controller. In other words, he gets rid of the nuisances.

Marc has served on the Savannah Jazz's board of directors and the Savannah Jazz festival committee and is in charge of logistics in the park every year at our annual festival. Thanks for everything, my "main man." Don't know what we would do without you.

Me and Howard (Howard Paul, guitarist, entrepreneur)

Howard Paul

Howard and I have advocated and collaborated on numerous jazz events. Since his arrival in Savannah in 1991, he has been a contributing force. He wears many hats that include president of Benedetto Guitars, past president of Savannah Jazz, and jazz promoter. Howard was inducted into the Savannah Jazz Hall of Fame in 2011.

Howard is also responsible for bringing numerous national jazz acts/performers to Savannah, and when he performs for any of the Savannah Jazz sponsored events, he does not accept a fee. We need more musicians and members like him. His resume of performances is impressive and includes Bob James, Joey DeFrancesco, Cyrus Chestnut, Tom Scott, and Ulysses Owens, naming just a few. It's a pleasure knowing, collaborating, and performing with him.

Me and Morgan (Morgan Guerin, multi-instrumentalist, producer, composer, engineer)

Morgan Guerin, Teddy Adams, Quentin Baxter

Prodigy is the most apt description of Morgan. He is the son of bassist Roland Guerin and obviously inherited a great deal of his father's genes. I met Morgan when he was in middle school. He became a regular in my annual "Future of Jazz" concert series during Black History Month. He could play John Coltrane's "Giant Steps" on tenor saxophone when I met him. Even more surprising to me was to find out that he was a multi-instrumentalist who could play all the saxophones, piano, bass drums, and EWI. His subsequent growth and development are astonishing.

One of the many things that amazed me the most about him was his humility. I observed with astonishment how he related and interacted with his peers, many his senior. He was just another youngster enjoying and exploring the wonders of this great art form called jazz.

I kept up with his success via the media, friends, and occasionally encountered his father, Roland. I was never surprised and always proud of him. It had been several years since we had seen each other, but at the 2023 Savannah Jazz Festival, he was performing with another rising star, flugel horn, and trumpet player, Milene Casada. He had also been touring with bassist Esperanza Spalding. It was great seeing him and catching up on what he had been doing, which was quite a lot.

Me and the Chef (Chef Joe Randal, Dean of Southern Cuisine)

Me and Chef Joe Randall

Some things are meant to happen (kismet). I have only known Chef Joe Randall for about five years, but it seems as if it has been much longer. The Chef is responsible for me being hired as musical director at Good Times Jazz Bar and Restaurant. Since our relationship began, it has developed into one of mutual admiration and respect. Putting it succinctly, in addition to being a chef who is featured in the culinary arts section of the Smithsonian's African American Museum of History and Culture, he is also a very hip dude.

Not only is he a well-read and knowledgeable man, but he also has both appreciation and respect for the great art form commonly referred to as jazz. I cannot identify a better person to work with regarding advocating and supporting jazz. He has given me his trust and does not hesitate presenting my suggestions, selection of artists, and proposals to the owners, Stephen and Danielle Moore.

He is a manager and consultant with a lot to say about managing a business and especially the people involved with it. As long as my ideas and dealing with the artists and club are feasible, he has my back, and I appreciate that more than he realizes. Since our relationship began, we have not only become cohorts, but we have also become friends.

The Chef is a very thorough and observant person who in many instances called my attention to things that I had forgotten or overlooked (of course with the most able assistance of his wife, Barbara). He is an asset to the club, restaurant, music, and musicians. Thank you, Chef Joe, for all you do.

Me and the Sextet (Eric Jones, Robert Saunders, Marc Chesanow, Calvin Barnes, Kirk Lee)

The Teddy Adams Sextet

The Eric Jones Trio (rhythm section for sextet)

Art Blakey and the Jazz Messengers is the main reason for me being partial to maintaining a sextet. He had several different musicians at various times, but each unit definitely brought something to the table. Finding regular gigs for six musicians is definitely a financial challenge, but the musical result is worth the effort and sacrifice.

I have been quite fortunate to have the Eric Jones Trio along with Kirk Lee and Calvin Barnes as regular, consistent, and capable members for several years now. Eric and Robert were profiled earlier in the book. The following pedigree amply describes the remaining members of the sextet.

Although Kirk Lee has a degree in engineering from the University of Mississippi, he is a most capable trumpet and flugel horn player. Since his arrival in Savannah more than thirty years ago, I have personally witnessed amazing development and understanding of the jazz concept. Not only is he an impressive improviser, but he also plays lead trumpet in the Savannah Jazz Orchestra. In addition to everything previously stated, Kirk is both agreeable and dependable. Now that's hard to beat.

Marc Chesanow is an extraordinary bass player. He received a BA in music from the Eastman School of Music and a Masters from the University of Memphis. He is comfortable playing almost any genre of music. In addition to being an in-demand bassist, he is also the principal bass violinist with the Savannah Philharmonic Symphony Orchestra. Marc is an impressive arranger and my go-to guy when I need music professionally printed. You see, I'm antiquated when it comes to technological savvy.

Dr. Calvin Barnes is well versed in two arenas. He graduated from Oberlin College with a double major, jazz studies, and premed. His medical degree is from Yale University's School of Medicine. Those accomplishments attest to him being both an impressive musician (clarinet, tenor, alto, and soprano saxophones) and medical doctor (radiologist). An ideal description of Calvin is succinctly this: a talented guy with love and understanding of this art form called jazz and a dedicated doctor who cares and is concerned about his patients. Now top those accolades.

I consider myself extremely fortunate to be associated and musically involved with these guys of this superlative caliber.

More "Conversations"

Pondering thoughts (me, Teddy Adams)

This section covers conversations I have had with several musicians including myself. Invariably, conversations and/or arguments arise regarding who the better or best jazz players or composers were and/or are, especially when comparing African Americans, Whites, and other musicians of color. During my periods of naivete, I would foolishly defend my opinion focusing on technique, ability, and concepts, not realizing that any musician who is dedicated to the art form and understands its theoretical concepts has something to offer regardless of race. I am embarrassed and want to literally crawl into a hole when I entertain that line of thought. I now realize why I prefer and relate to the African American creative expression without dealing with *better or best* comparison.

The best comprehensive explanation was and is very obvious and simplistic. African American creative expression is different. The adjective *different* negates any futile attempt to compare ability, etc. The creative expression of African Americans in music and especially the art form commonly referred to as jazz is based on their lives and experiences, thereby culminating in an individual and collective creative process. Whether embracing ancestral connections through cultural memory or experiencing life in its present state, the creative expression is different and can only be emulated by others.

The art form commonly referred to as jazz is musically infinite. It represents freedom and since freedom/equality has always and still does elude African Americans, the innate voice of musical expression rendered by them is unique and honest because of this deprivation. Once again, cultural memory is inherent and not imputed. It's simply a fact of life.

What is jazz? The art form commonly referred to as jazz is the most profound creatively expressed music in existence. The term jazz is a misguided, mislabeled, and misleading label applied to an art form that is misunderstood and underappreciated for its substance and infinity.

Milt Hinton, "The Judge"

Milt Hinton was one of the most amicable and down-to-earth musicians that I have ever encountered. When you consider his ability on the bass (slap-bass-style pioneer) and his achievements in photography, that makes him a very special guy. During a conversation with Milt at a friend's house (jazz enthusiast, Henry Moore), he shared this important trivia with me.

When I asked how he managed to break the color barrier by becoming one of the first established studio staff musicians, he gave a lot of the credit to entertainer, comedian, and actor Jackie Gleason. According to Milt, during a slow period for gigs, he encountered Jackie while walking to a rehearsal in New York. He had worked with Jackie before, so Jackie was well aware of his status as being a consummate bassist. Milt shared that gigs were slow and he was in need of work. Jackie then invited him to do a recording session at Radio City.

When Milt showed up for the session, he was told that they already had a bass player. However, when Jackie arrived, he matter-of-factly stated, "Now you have two bass players." As a result of that incident, Milt became a much sought-after studio musician for many years to come.

Ben Riley, drummer (The Up of the Down Beat)

During our friendship, Ben and I shared many varied and interesting conversations. Most of the time, it was Ben who was imparting, and I was listening and absorbing. I can recall the following tidbits that stuck with me. Of course, these are in addition to those shared in *The Up of the Down Beat*. According to Ben, he, Sahib Shihab (Edmund Gregory), and James Moody had known each other for years, conversing and playing together, and did not realize that all three of them were from Savannah, Georgia. Ben claimed New York (Sugar Hill); Moody claimed Newark, New Jersey; and Sahib just didn't claim anywhere. Subsequent to that revelation, whenever they encountered one another, they fondly called each other Homeboy.

One year at the Savannah Jazz Festival (2005), we featured "Women In Jazz," and both Cindy Blackman and Kim Thompson performed. After we had heard both of them play, Ben leaned toward me and whispered, "Cindy plays her a—— off, but Kim swings better." Of course, Kim was one of his mentees, and she could really swing. I experienced that at the jam session later that night when she and Tia Fuller sat in with my group.

Ben recalled the last time he encountered Max Roach, his mentor and idol, before Max stopped playing. "We had lunch, and after, as he walked away, I could tell by the way he was walking that it was just a matter of time before he would no longer be able to continue playing."

That reminded me of Art "Bu" Blakey. During his later years, when he started to lose his hearing, he was relying greatly on floor vibrations but still swinging his a—— off.

Norman Tucker, trumpet player

Norman Tucker is a trumpet player who I met while living in Tokyo. He was from Los Angeles and had very good taste when choosing tunes that he wanted to play. My song repertoire was enhanced because of him. He shared with me two unusual experiences that I still think and laugh about.

Norman studied with Joe Gordon, an outstanding trumpet player during the fifties and sixties who was making a name for himself but, because of drug use, tragically burned himself up while smoking in bed before achieving success. He had played with Art

Blakey, Charlie Parker, Lionel Hampton, Thelonious Monk, and many others. According to Norman, his lessons consisted of Joe borrowing his trumpet (he used his mouthpiece) and walking around the room playing nonstop for about thirty minutes. Norman said that his ideas were both hip and endless.

This ritual happened at each lesson. When he finished, perhaps from fatigue, he abruptly stopped playing and extended his hand to Norman with the same accompanying statement: "That was your lesson. Where is my money?" Norman also told me about going to his last lesson and finding Joe locked in his small apartment and could not get out. He fabricated a story and convinced Norman to break the lock from the outside and, upon entering, borrowed Norman's shoes to run an errand. Tucker later found out that Joe's girlfriend had locked him in the room and taken his shoes so that he would not go out and score drugs. Norman never saw him again and had to go home without any shoes. Now, that's hilarious.

Norman also studied with tenor saxophonist extraordinaire Harold Land (best known for his stint with trumpeter Clifford Brown). According to Norman, Harold Land was living quite comfortably in a nice area with a swimming pool and other luxuries. He gave lessons at his home. Norman and Harold became friends, and Norman would sometimes babysit and perform certain chores around the house, which included cleaning the swimming pool. He said he was never paid any money and had to pay Harold for each and every lesson. Wow, I guess business is business.

Bob Faircloth, advocate/supporter

Me and Bob Faircloth

During a recent interview with Bob Faircloth, this writer found him to be a very interesting person with quite an impressive jazz history. The following is a synopsis of that interview.

Successful businessman, world traveler, and philanthropic advocate for the arts are just some of the attributes describing Bob Faircloth. Originally from Canada and a resident of several other countries and US locations, Bob is now a resident of Savannah, Georgia, and one of the best blessings that has been bestowed upon the arts community, especially the jazz arena.

Born in the 1930s, Bob has been in the presence of jazz most of his life, which includes early musical experiences with both the piano and saxophone. This first at-length conversation with him convinced me that he has a passion for jazz that dates as far back as The Jazz at the Philharmonics. I was impressed with his knowledge of the music and, in spite of his extensive business career, his appreciation and support of it. We shared a lot of common experiences in our jazz exposure. Talking with him was almost like conversing with another musician about jazz. His appreciation and comprehension are unquestionable.

During the years that he has lived in Savannah, his financial support of the arts with special emphasis on jazz organizations, i.e., the Savannah Music Festival and the Savannah Jazz Association, is immeasurable, Jazz's patron saint. Bob has forged relationships with many musicians and emphasizes his association with two worthy individuals in the persons of pianists Marcus Roberts and the late Ben Tucker. Yours truly proudly boasts a recent budding relationship with Bob and am sure that it will continue because of our commitment to this great art form commonly referred to as jazz.

I was quite pleased to play a small part in his induction into the 2022 Savannah Jazz Hall of Fame. I say small part because his selection was unanimous. It was a pleasure sharing our thoughts on jazz, and I'm sure that the future will allow us to do great things for this profound art form that America has given to the world.

*Willie Draper, Big Black (*The Up of the Down Beat*)*

According to conversations with Willie Draper and Big Black, Savannahian William "Fish" Ray was an unsung hero who, although not a jazz musician, helped perpetuate Savannah's jazz legacy. His professional name was Fish Ray, and he made a name for himself in the calypso music genre. For many years, he was a member of the Lord Flea calypso band, an internationally recognized group that was featured on many major stages including the *Ed Sullivan Show.*

While living in Savannah, Fish established a reputation as being a musical entrepreneur who mastered hand drums and introduced the tub bass (a tin wash tub turned upside down with a stick and cord attached to it). The tub bass produced different tones by manipulating the stick and cord. Draper once told me that you could actually hear the bass notes to the chord changes. Fish maintained a band that consisted of several pieces with arrangements. The band performed concerts and played for dances.

Big Black, who is Fish's younger brother, gives him credit for being a great influence in his development. Fish made Big Black's first drum and is responsible for him moving to Miami where his career began its formulation.

Draper stated that Fish was quite a hustler and kept his band exposed and working regularly while living in Savannah. This writer never had the experience of playing with Fish but met and hung with him several times. He and my mentor, Willie Draper, were very good friends.

Ben Riley

Ben Riley (Note about Monk and Coltrane)

Drummer extraordinaire Ben Riley (featured in *The Up of the Down Beat*) and I had many interesting and informative conversations over the many years that I knew him. I have shared some of them in my first book. The following trivia comes to mind, and I could not resist sharing it with you.

According to Ben, there was a period of woodshedding/rehearsing when Monk and Trane religiously spent the entire day, every day, playing Monk's music and discussing intricacies and theory of music in general. It seems as if a beginning time was established, 8:00 a.m., but not an ending time. Monk's piano was next to his apartment's door entrance. Ben said that every day at 8:00 a.m. sharp, Monk would open his door, and Trane would walk through horn in hand.

There was never any notification or knocking at the door before entering. Monk would automatically open the door, and Trane would enter the apartment. This was a daily ritual.

When I heard the recording of Monk and Trane live at Carnegie Hall, that ritual was quite evident in their playing. I have never heard anything like it. It was evident that they had spent a lot of time together.

James Moody

Savannah's own James Moody

James Moody ("Conversations," *The Up of the Down Beat*) and I talked a lot about music and musicians whenever we encountered one another. After several meetings, he, Ben Riley, Eddie Pazant, and I fondly referred to one another as homeboy. I remember a particular conversation when we talked about the difficulty of playing some tunes and how reading rather than hearing them could sometimes save time until they were committed to memory. Moody hesitated and looked at me with a smile and said, "Man, I thought I could read music until I moved to Las Vegas and started playing those different shows. I found out that I didn't read as well as I thought I did. Playing Vegas was a rude awakening but a great and needed learning experience."

Unforgettables, Regrettables, and Destiny

This section entitled "Unforgettables, Regrettables, and Destiny" is a continuation of the encounters and experiences covered in *The Up of the Down Beat*, but this time included are regrets and in, some instances, results and consequences. Some incidents are hilarious and others thought-provoking and enlightening. Aspects of life that include success, sadness, happiness, accomplishments, and realism all combine to leave indelible impressions in my life.

I envy the person who can truthfully say, "If I had my life to live again, I wouldn't change a thing," and I certainly can empathize with the person who would change many things. Life is like syncopation in music, sometimes difficult to read or play but necessary to achieve our desired outcome.

Betrayed by his hometown

During the mid-eighties, trombonist Trummy Young returned to the states from living in Hawaii for a brief concert tour. He played Atlanta and Macon, Georgia. The Coastal Jazz Association (now Savannah Jazz) was contacted to see if he could perform in Savannah. Let's consider these important known facts: Trummy Young was a Savannahian. He was a great trombonist/vocalist who had performed with Jimmy Lunceford and Charlie Parker and had the distinction of playing with Louis Armstrong longer than any other trombonist.

To my dismay and disappointment, the Coastal Jazz Association, Savannah's jazz representation, did not take advantage of the offer at a cost of only $500. The disappointment I experienced almost caused me to depart from the organization. I resented it then and feel the same now. In spite of my disappointment, I considered that its advocacy for the support and perpetuation of jazz was more important than my personal feelings.

Small in size but big otherwise

My high school classmate and fellow musician and above all quite a character was named William Lonon (deceased), aka The Midget or, as he referred to himself, Sugar Dick Bill. William was a small person, about four feet or less tall, but his ego, tall tales, and, from what I gather, private part were anything but small. Of course, we only called him Midget behind his back because he was known to carry his 38 pistol at all times and did not hesitate to threaten using it on anyone who rubbed him wrong, women included.

William played guitar (more of a blues than jazz player) but knew some jazz tunes and licks. I returned to Savannah in 1976 after living in Asia almost twelve years. I encountered William at a club one night. He had just returned from residing in Boston for several years. It was rather dark in the club, and he did not recognize me at first; after all, we hadn't seen each other for more than fifteen years. Of course, he was pretty easy to recognize, so during our conversation, I asked if he was still playing, and he boldly stated, "What else do you think I would be doing?"

To that I countered with "I guess you're playing your a——off now."

He then countered with "If you have heard George Benson, you've heard me."

I was lost for words. Of course I knew better because I remember what his capability was the last time I heard him, and I seriously doubted if he had developed to that level. He further relayed some of his exploits while living in Boston, which included sharing an apartment with George Benson (he and George exchanged ideas and licks) and being married to a six-feet-tall blond with blue eyes. I later learned the latter to be true because she had visited Savannah with him and I had a friend, drummer Herbie King (*The Up of the Down Beat*) who knew her.

William did not actually realize who I was until a few days later when we met during the day. I immediately saw the surprised look on his face when he finally recognized me and blurted out, "Oh, man, it's you, Teddy. I didn't recognize you the other night."

I simply countered with "I know you didn't."

Since I had just gotten back in town myself, I assembled a group of musicians to find out what I was working with. The Midget was one of the musicians. One rehearsal made my mind up about who I was not going to be using in my band. Needless to say, one of them was the Midget.

After calling a blues or two, I suggested "Blue Bossa," by trumpeter Kenny Dorham. Not a hard tune, but there is a key change after eight bars of the tune, and you have to know the tune to play it correctly. Every time we got to the ninth bar, the Midget would play the wrong chord changes. Finally, I approached him and told him that he was playing the wrong chord changes to which he looked me squarely in my eyes and boldly stated, "I know it, but my changes will fit," and that was the end of our conversation and also our music relationship. In spite of that, we remained friends and maintained a good relationship because he knew that I knew what time it was— what a character. I still laugh when I think about it.

The all-time longest migraine headaches

I am a member of a breakfast club that meets weekly. It's a socio/civic group of old friends who gather for the sake of sharing camaraderie and supporting worthwhile community organizations. From time to time, conference calls are made to old friends, and everyone would reminisce about nostalgic past events and experiences. This particular morning, we connected with a former neighborhood friend and schoolmate who I had known all of my childhood. His name was Earl, and I had not seen or talked to him about forty years.

It was great recalling certain memories, and all of a sudden, he told me to shut up because he wanted to get something off of his chest. I immediately became concerned, and then, he let me have it. "Man, are you still playing the trombone?" I answered him with a resounding yes. He paused and stated with an exaggerated groan. "Man, I still suffer from migraine headaches because of all that noise you used to make when you practiced." He then started to horribly mimic the sound of the trombone or should I say elephant because that's what he sounded like.

Everyone got a big laugh out of that. I couldn't stop laughing because that was funny. What an unusual way to remember our childhood, but I did practice every day, and I'm sure both he and the neighborhood got tired of all that noise.

The hardest taskmaster ever

My mentor, friend, and musician/saxophonist extraordinaire Willie Draper ("Me and the Cats," *The Up of the Down Beat*) was the hardest teacher I ever experienced. I met him in 1956 and began hanging and studying with him in 1957.

Draper died on August 14, 2010. Our relationship of 54 years yielded only four compliments from him. The first time he heard me play was in the band room at my high school. He showed me a bass line that was featured in a *DownBeat* magazine. It consisted of mostly quarter notes, so it was not difficult to play. When I finished playing it after some interruptions and phasing corrections, he stated, "Yeah, you got a pretty good and big sound on that horn."

After playing with him for a while, he nonchalantly looked at me and said, "I think you're strong enough for me to start writing and arranging like I really want to. You've been riding shotgun long enough." A few years later he, with a half-smile on his face, said, "You will probably turn out to be a pretty good bullsh——t trombone player."

Much later in our relationship, after hearing a recording of me and one of his colleagues who also played saxophone (he was never overly impressed with his playing ability), he turned to me and said,

"Man, I'm glad you were on that recording because you saved it." That was the highest praise that he had ever bestowed upon me.

All of the other conversations through the years regarding my trombone playing were in the form of critiques, which included criticism, advice, challenges, and/or information that he felt I should know. I'm still forever grateful for his veracity.

The hardest gig I ever played

Sometime in early 1982, the exact time escapes me now. The Ringling Bros. and Barnum & Bailey Circus came to Savannah. This event was special and happened fairly often. I don't recall if it was an annual event or not, but they contacted the local musicians' union (AFM 447-704) regarding musicians to play four performances over a two-day period. This gig consisted of a rehearsal plus the performances. Gigs were slow, and I had never either played or seen a live circus, so I agreed to do the gig. This was definitely an unforgettable gig. I should have suspected that something was unusual when I heard that it traveled with two lead trumpet players.

I should have quit after the rehearsal because it was so grueling. The music was difficult, and things were moving so rapidly that there was barely enough time to breathe and turn the pages of the music. I was so exhausted after each performance that all I wanted to do was go somewhere and lay down and rest. I can't ever recall being so tired after playing a performance. A friend of mine, trumpeter Joey Waters, blew his chops (lips) out, to the point of them bleeding before we completed the last performance. To add insult to injury, I still didn't actually see or enjoy the circus. I was too busy reading the dots (music). When the circus came to town again, I was not gigging anywhere, but I refused that gig. Now that wasn't funny then, and I find it hard to laugh about it now. But I guess I can because I survived it, definitely a lesson learned and an experience that was never or will ever be repeated.

Busted on the bandstand

Bassist Ben Tucker ("Me and the Cats," *The Up of the Down Beat*) owned the hippest jazz club in Savannah named Hard Hearted Hannah's (after a song written about a Savannah female). We had some great jam sessions and gigs there. One night, I was doing a gig along with his trio that included a fabulous pianist named Joe "Virginia" Jones, and a very hip drummer, who I had met years earlier when I was a teenager, named Ron Free. Needless to say, it was a very strong trio. All three of those cats had played with a host of elite national musicians. Someone called "So What," a tune by Miles Davis. It's a bass feature. It's also a modal tune with only two chord changes, D minor and E flat minor. It's not a hard tune, but playing the melody a half step up from where you started (a modulation) can be tricky if you don't play it often. Ben Tucker had not played it in a while, so the modulation gave him a little trouble. He fumbled every time he played the modulated section.

No one said anything for a while after we finished playing the tune, that is, no one but Ron Free, who could and would say some interesting things sometimes. Ron leaned toward Ben and said, "So Ben, what was that 'Guess What?'" We, the band, laughed our behinds off, and Ben got his jaws tight (mad). Now that was funny then, and it's still funny now.

Simultaneously surprised and intimidated

Charleston, South Carolina, annually hosts one of the best musical festivals in the country known as Spoleto. It's an eclectic music festival that includes outstanding jazz performances. In addition to Spoleto, there is also Piccolo Spoleto, which is all jazz and focuses a great deal on local and regional acts. I have had the privilege of performing at Piccolo Spoleto several times. Drummer and friend Ron Free was responsible for my initial appearance in the early nineties.

My quintet included Ron on drums, Tommy Gill piano, Delbert Felix bass, and a very fine tenor saxophonist Howard Nicholson. It was a very strong group, and we were very well received. As I previously mentioned, I performed at several festivals, and the last one included pianist Doug Carn, Delbert Felix, and Drummer Eric Vaughn.

The second night of performing, I happened to look toward one of the front tables, and to my surprise, sitting there were none other than two fine trombonists, George Bohanon and Maurice Spears who were performing with the Horace River Septet. I don't know whether I played well or not. I did the best that I could considering the pressure that I felt. They were gracious with their compliments, and we hung out and had a great time. We were also invited to the Horace Silver concert the next night. Of course, it was out of sight. A few years later, George Bohanon and I got a chance to play together on Hilton Head Island while he was on vacation. We had a mutual friend, pianist Jimmy Minger ("Me and the Cats," *The Up of the Down Beat*). Of course, I enjoyed it, probably more than he did—a very nice cat who can play his a—— off.

Being shamed served its purpose

My first private lessons really made an indelible impression on me. I was fifteen years old, and my teacher was an outstanding trumpet player named Bernie Franklin. He was stationed at the local air force base in Savannah and was one of the featured trumpet players in the Air Force band. Bernie introduced me to aspects of playing that I was never made aware of such as buzzing, proper tonguing, diaphragmatic breathing, and other important things that I needed to know and had never been taught.

He was a very dedicated and serious teacher. I can vividly recall this incident as if it was yesterday instead of sixty-five years ago. I arrived at one of my weekly lessons (only $2 per lesson) and had not practiced my assignment. About three or four minutes of playing made it very clear that I had not practiced. Bernie gave me a disgusted stare and boldly stated, "Here is your money, man. You haven't practiced this music, and I refuse to take your money. Come back next week when you are ready." I never forgot that, and I was never unprepared again. Thank you for caring, Bernie.

The Real McCoy

I think the year was 1972. I was living in Tokyo, perhaps one of the most important periods in my life. You can never tell because I'm still alive and experiencing the unexpected. My best friend and one of the best pianist that I have ever known, heard, or played with, Takehiro Honda ("The Japan Scene/Unforgettables," *The Up of the Down Beat*), and I hung out a lot when we were not gigging. We attended a lot of jazz concerts because we were not charged the usual cover cost. We were checking McCoy Tyler out at one of his many concerts. He came to Japan a lot. The Japanese were crazy about him.

During the concert, the band, which consisted of Sonny Fortune, Alphonse Mouzan, and Alex Blake, if I recall because I saw him a number of times, left the bandstand, and an ancient Japanese string instrument called the koto was brought to the stage. My friend, Takehiro Honda or Honda-san as I called him, leaned over and informed me that it was a gift the Japanese people had given him when he was playing with John Coltrane.

Everyone eagerly awaited his performance on this authentic ancient instrument. To my surprise and Honda-san's along with the Japanese audience, we were blown away by what we heard. According to Honda-san, he played it with the finesse of someone who had been exposed to it for years. Once again, McCoy had overwhelmed me as well as everyone with his genius, truly unforgettable.

Overdue tribute

Ben Riley, drummer extraordinaire, was born in Savannah and went on to become one of the most recorded and appreciated drummers in modern jazz. He performed and/or recorded with many of the jazz greats such as Thelonious Monk, Sonny Rollins, Eddie "Lock Jaw" Davis, Johnny Griffin, and Alice Coltrane, to name only a few. He died in 2017, and other than a small tribute held in Wyandanch,

New York (Long Island), a proper tribute recognizing his greatness was never held.

In 2018, I proposed a proper tribute to the Coastal Jazz Association (now Savannah Jazz) for him. The organization non-hesitantly agreed. The 36th Annual Savannah Jazz Festival was dedicated to Ben. For that special event, I composed a tribute song entitled "Big Ben," the name his wife, Inez, often called him. I chose three drummers for the tribute: Quentin Baxter, Robert Boone, and Sean Bolden. Each drummer played on certain tunes during the set, and all three of them played on his tribute tune.

It was an outstanding performance consisting of a serious duel of friendly competition and well received and appreciated by the audience (Forsyth Park was packed to its capacity). Present at the tribute were Ben's wife, Inez, and his children, who consisted of four generations of Rileys. Ben's son Jay came to me after the performance and extended his sincerest appreciation. Needless to say, his wife, Inez, was overwhelmed. Humbled, I was glad to have been able to orchestrate and succeed in this endeavor.

He really dug Savannah

Every year, the big band the Savannah Jazz Orchestra, which I co-lead with saxophonist Randy Reese, accompanies a featured guest performer at the Savannah Jazz Festival. I have forgotten the year, but we backed vocalist Ernie Andrews, one of my favorite singers. It was a great performance, and Ernie was scheduled to leave Savannah the next morning. His ticket had already been purchased.

About a week later, I was playing a gig at one of the local clubs and who strolls in with a lady on each arm but Ernie Andrews as high as a Georgia pine tree. He sat in with the band and sang a few tunes. We had a very hip set, and I did not see him again. I have no idea when he left Savannah.

Several years later, he appeared at the Savannah Jazz Festival with the Harper Brothers Band. We laughed and joked about his previous trip to Savannah, but this time, he departed the next day as scheduled. Now that was funny then, and it's still funny now.

Bebop as a spoken language

At the 1985 Savannah Jazz Festival, two of the headliners were Lionel Hampton and Betty "Bebop" Carter. Of course, Betty Carter got her nickname Bebop because of her improvisational scat singing. She would scat sing as if she was playing an instrument or maybe as if she was an instrument. She did her set before Lionel Hampton's orchestra played. I was sitting in front of the bandstand with friends, and Betty was in rear form. Accompanying her was a very young but talented trio led by an up and coming pianist named Benny Green. My friend's son was intrigued by what he was witnessing. He was all of five or six years old. Betty Carter was mesmerizing him with her scat singing. After about two songs, he leaned over toward his Dad and, with a very serious look on his face, asked, "So, Dad, what is that language that she is singing in?" I was lost for words. That was honest and funny then, and it is hilarious now.

Sometimes, it pays to be a rookie

The year was 1957, and I was sixteen years old. It was my junior year in high school, and I was fortunate enough to be playing with my high school band director and organist, James Drayton ("Conversations," *The Up of the Down Beat*). I was the youngster in the band and was proud and glad to be playing with my mentors. Everybody in there was an experienced professional and had taken me under their wings because they knew I was serious and eager to learn.

This was my first experience playing with seasoned musicians who included Bobby Dilworth on alto sax and flute, Alfonso Frasier trumpet, Thurlow Scott bass, and Ray Lewis drums and also experiencing the thrill of playing a well-rehearsed Broadway-style floor show with dancers, comedians, singers, and the usual other special features. The show was called the *Phil Harris Review*. Phil was a master entertainer who worked out of Miami, Florida, and was known for always producing spectacular events. What an experience and thrill for a teenager. Being the rookie in the band, naturally, I was also the errand boy. All the female dancers called me Junior, and I didn't mind it at all.

Every night, it was my job to keep up with and notify the acts before they came on. Just by chance one night, I entered the dressing room to notify the dancers that it was their time. I forgot to knock, and when I opened the door, I got an eyeful of naked and/or partially naked women. They got quite a laugh out of my reaction, and I got quite a reaction out of myself. Standing there with my eyes stretched, a dumbfounded facial expression, and a bulge in my pants must have been quite a sight. They had a ball teasing me after that, but you better believe that I never knocked again and enjoyed every minute of being the errand boy. I realized that the earlier I came to notify them, the more of an eyeful I got. That was the highlight of the night for me.

What a reunion

I played with the Charleston Jazz Orchestra for five years ("Bands and Organizations," *The Up of the Down Beat*). It was a wonderful experience, and its director, Charlton Singleton, did a fine job at the helm. As covered in my first book, *The Up of the Down Beat*, I lived in Charleston for three years prior to going to Viet Nam. It was a memorable sojourn, and I enjoyed playing with the musicians there who I knew because my mentor, Willie Draper, had proceeded me and given me the names of the cats who could play and I needed to look up. One in particular was alto saxophonist Oscar Rivers.

Oscar, like Draper, loved bebop and had studied with Draper just as I had. We were very close in age and had a lot in common, mainly the friendship and mentorship of Willie Draper. At a special Charleston Jazz Orchestra Concert, the band featured Oscar playing the music of Charlie Parker with strings. Members of the Charleston Symphony were added for the final needed touch. I invited Draper to accompany me to the concert because Oscar was the feature and they had not seen each other in almost fifty years.

I will never forget the scene after the concert. Draper came backstage to congratulate Oscar who had no idea that he was in the audience. Fifty years of emotion culminated with embraces, tears, and, above all, mentor/mentee pride. I was as caught up in the moment as they were, an indelible memory.

"Death, I ain't scared of you"

The following dispositions of friends, musicians, and family who were confronted with the inevitability of departing this planet varied but lucidly reflected their intrepid acceptance of the imminency. I truly envy them and hope that if faced with a synonymous posture, I can be equally at peace.

During my sojourn on this earth, I have encountered five people who were not afraid to die. Two of them were family members, my mother and older brother. My mother decided she was ready for death when my father passed. They had known each other all of their cognizant life and married for fifty-six years. She believed in God and the hereafter and wanted to join her friend, husband, and, I truly believe, the only man she had known in her life. Every year, the family would attend the church anniversary where she was baptized as a child and where both she and my father are buried side by side. She would go to his gravesite, bow her head, and stand there until I would go to her and reluctantly tell her that it was time to leave. Invariably, when I asked her what she was doing or thinking, I got the same reply: "Just talking to your Daddy and telling him that I would be seeing him soon." That brought tears to my eyes every time.

My brother, Lonnie, confided to me shortly before he passed that he was ready to depart because he had been ill for quite a while, and as he stated, "I'm ready to go home." He really touched and surprised me when he said that because I had never thought of him as being religious.

Pianist Joe Jones ("Conversations," *The Up of the Down Beat*) appeared to be at peace with departing this planet. One day while visiting him, he asked if I could cop some drugs for him. According to Joe, it certainly did not make a difference at this stage in his life. He was dying from stage 4 cancer. I cleared it with his wife, Debra, and did as he requested. Thereafter, every time I saw him, he was sitting up in the hospital-style bed that had been furnished by the medical support people and holding onto an attached harness for support. According to his wife, Debra, whenever she entered his room, he was holding onto the harness as if he was holding onto life, but not afraid to depart from it.

Frank Drayton was a pianist and friend from high school. He was also the son of my third director and mentor, James Drayton. Frank returned to Savannah after years of being away. He had been sick for a while and was on social security disability. He asked me to be his guarantor and receive his disability checks, which I did without hesitation. I later found out that he had been diagnosed with stage 4 cancer.

I would see him regularly, and it was evident that the cancer was taking a toll on him. One day, he called and told me that he had something he wanted to share with me. We sat in his room at the subsidized facility where he resided, and he confided to me that the chemo treatments that he was undergoing had become intolerable and he was going to discontinue them. That was quite a shock to me. I couldn't imagine what I would have done if I was faced with a similar dilemma.

We decided on a date, and I took him to the bus station because he had decided to go live with his mother until the time of departure came. Frank was not raised by her. He always lived with his grandmother, but she welcomed him when he needed her. About two months after we last saw one another, I got a thank you card from his mother informing me of his demise. I often pondered and tried to empathize with his situation but always found it difficult to fathom. It saddened me then, and it still does now.

Last, but certainly not least, was a saxophonist introduced to me by pianist and friend Claude Rhea ("Me and the 'Cats,'" *The Up of the Down Beat*). It pains me not to recall his name because we shared a special bond for only a short period of time, but I will never ever forget him. When I started this writing adventure, I realized that I had forgotten his name and that everyone that I knew who knew him, including Claude, was no longer existing in this life, very sad.

He had been diagnosed with terminal cancer (this curse has taken so many) and given only a few weeks to live. Claude always considered me as one of his true mentors and wanted the two of us to meet because he felt that we had a lot in common. He was absolutely right. We only met in person one time for an entire day. Subsequently, we communicated by phone regularly. We talked about music, life, death, and whatever else that came to mind. I feel that our meeting one another was kismet.

I really appreciated the peace and acceptance of death that he shared. I still envy him for his attitude and contentment. We covered a lot of ground in a very short period of time. It was as if we had known each other for a lifetime. He slipped away peacefully and quietly. I still remember him as if it was yesterday, which brings to mind an old African adage: "A man is not dead as long as he is remembered. His spirit remains amongst us." His spirit is still with me even though I can't recall his name. Rest in peace, my brother, and thank you, Claude Rhea, for having the inner foresightedness to realize that this union should happen.

Young, foolish, and lucky

A memorable, dangerous, and unbelievable incident happened in 1957 while the high school dance band that I was playing with ventured on a road tour with blues singer Jimmy Liggins ("Unforgettables," *The Up of the Down Beat*). The band was out of school on summer break, and we were on the so-called Chittlin' Circuit. We played in a small town in Georgia by the name of Moulrie. It had only one black club that was capable of presenting live acts. I later found out from my pianist, Eric Jones, who is from Moultrie, that his grandmother recalls that it was the American Legion.

I remember arriving at the club in the early evening before the gig started. I remember drinking, eating, and meeting some young ladies. By the time the gig started, we had become quite friendly with some of the ladies, and our piano player, Frank Drayton, had made quite an impression on one of them. During the gig that night, she was on the bandstand sitting next to Frank at the piano. We soon found out that she was spoken for because a dude came to the club looking for her, saw her sitting next to Frank on the piano bench, pulled out a gun, and shot toward the bandstand, grazing his lady in the arm. Of course, that cleared the bandstand. All of us immediately vacated it. As a matter of fact, it cleared the club.

After things were quelled, the festivities began again as if nothing had happened, and you probably won't believe this because had I not seen it, I would not have believed it. To our astonishment, the same chick who had just been shot in the arm was not only back in the club but once again sitting next to Frank on the piano bench with a piece of cloth tied around the gunshot wound. The rest of the night was, to say the least, quite uneasy. Fortunately, nothing happened. We never saw her boyfriend again, and Frank was still in hot pursuit of her. Now, was that insane, or what?

Where did he put it?

During one of the jazz festivals, Slide Hampton conducted a masterclass at Armstrong State University (now Georgia Southern University). During the class, the band was playing some of his music, and the lead alto player was having a little difficulty reading it. Slide gave him some clarification by transposing and playing it on the trombone. I had noticed that while teaching the class, Slide was chewing gum, not unusual because I have seen trombone players chew gum before when they were playing, including myself, but they, as well as I, would stop chewing the gum and conveniently stick it to the trombone weight balance attached to the bell of the horn, a common practice; however, Slide did not do this. He never took it out of his mouth, and when he finished playing, he began chewing it again. I was amazed, but I never tried to do it.

He stole a lot from my mentor

While living in Tokyo, I got a chance to meet, hang out, and play with quite a few outstanding musicians. Freddie Hubbard brought a group to Japan that included Junior Cook on tenor saxophone. He had just replaced Joe Henderson. He found out that I was from Savannah and my mentor was Willie Draper, which prompted him to tell me how much he learned from Draper and how fortunate he was to have encountered him. As he put it, "If he farted, I sniffed." We both got a big laugh out of that.

Do as I say, not as I do

One of my biggest regrets is not taking formal piano lessons. When I first started in music, my focus was on playing a horn without anticipating a future career in music and the importance of the piano. I thought that my involvement in music would probably end when I finished high school. Little did I know at that time that it would be a lifelong passion.

Not only did I talk my parents into buying a used piano, but I also convinced them that my little sister, the baby and a girl, should learn piano, so it was purchased with her in mind. I focused on the saxophone and later the trombone without thinking seriously about the piano but instead encouraged my sister to take it seriously. I did not realize how important the piano was until I became interested in playing jazz and encountered chord changes.

In addition to the aforementioned, I now realize that the piano is indispensable when it comes to arranging and composing. Equally as important is the working and/or gigging opportunities. I have since gained a functional ability, but, man, do I wish that I could really play the piano.

The hard taskmaster

I insisted that my kids be involved in music because by the time they were of age, I had become a dedicated and serious musician. All three of them played piano and several instruments. Unfortunately, when I realized that they had the talent, I became overbearingly demanding. They excelled beyond my expectations, and my tyrannical approach to requiring them to practice and produce was a definite turnoff to them. I literally turned them against wanting to pursue an extended interest in performing. I could not help myself. They had incredible talent. Whether it was environmental, innate, or generic, I'm not sure, but it was there.

They were among the best in piano and band. My oldest, Tatia, had already started to accompany me on various programs, and my son Chance was demonstrating the ability to learn licks and cliches that I showed him. My baby, Traci, did what she saw her siblings do. They all were gifted, but the "ole dad" turned them off and away. I truly regret that.

Destiny is unpredictable but inevitable

Although I failed to lure them toward music as performers, a thorough understanding and appreciation definitely remained. My son is dabbling in creating beats for hip-hop, and both of my daughters are two of the highest-ranking females in the music/entertainment national arena. They are double minorities, African American and female. My oldest grandson Tad is a promising guitarist (also an engineer), and my middle granddaughter is a self-taught pianist who has the ability to hear very difficult and intricate jazz lines and passages and play them. She played "Central Park West" by John Coltrane at my eightieth birthday party (with a rhythm section). There must be some truth to genetic acquirement because although I spent time with them and they were exposed to music in a limited manner, they both show the same exceptional music ability that my kids, their parents, possessed.

If only Bangkok had developed faster

After spending three years in Bangkok, I was satisfied with everything but the music scene. Had that been hipper, I probably would not have left. The music scene there was tolerable but not satisfying enough to motivate me to remain. I met my wife there, and other things, if you get my drift, were overwhelmingly tolerable. Had I been clairvoyant or farsighted, perhaps I would have remained and tried to help develop a real jazz environment. The Filipinos had somewhat of a monopoly, but it was not solid enough to keep me there, especially with a possible return to Tokyo, Japan, on the horizon. Of course, I don't regret returning to Tokyo, but over the years, Bangkok has gained a jazz music conservatory, several venues, and an annual jazz festival. I guess I should have been more optimistic considering that the king at that time, Bhumibol Adulyadej, was a jazz musician and Lionel Hampton did an annual tour and royal jam session there. As it is said, "Hindsight is 20/20 vision." Not remaining is one of my biggest regrets. My wife still has relatives there, so my family and I visit Thailand every other year.

An unexpected observation and flattering compliment

I can vividly recall playing a gig at a club in Thunderbolt, Georgia, a suburb of Savannah (Savannah State University is located there). The band was on break when one of the patrons who had been sitting and attentively listening and appreciating the music approached me. She introduced herself, Daphne Jackson, and expressed how much she liked jazz and the set that we had just finished. She then said something that I did not expect from the average listener, "Man, I dig the way you play the trombone. You remind me of my favorite trombone player, a cat by the name of Benny Green." I was humbled and lost for words because except for some of the musicians that I played with, I didn't realize that a random listener would detect that. You see, Benny Green was my first influence. I liked what he played, and stealing his licks, cliches, and solos was attainable. My approach to improvising was and still is influenced by his style of playing. Daphne and I became friends, and she was always very supportive of me as a musician. I later found out that she had a son named Jeffery who played trumpet and congas.

Jeff, although much younger, and I became friends and shared a mentor/mentee relationship. He subsequently majored in music in college and became a band director. He and I even played some gigs together. I saw him recently at a club that I was playing, and he told me that he was holding a retirement party, my how time flies, which also means that I'm getting older.

It's never too late to change your mind

Me and "Perky"

As stated in my previous book, *The Up of the Down Beat*, I lean more toward playing with other instrumentalists than vocalists, but of course, I certainly appreciate good singers. Since the release of the aforementioned book, I have had the privilege of meeting and performing with three exceptional standouts in the persons of Dred "Perky" Scott, Cynthia Utterbach, and Nicolas Bearde. Each one of them is uniquely different but brings a lot to the table.

Perky Scott, who is also a lawyer and minister, is superb when it comes to maintaining the essence of jazz doing his performance as well as being equally entertaining. His performances are somewhat of a continuation of his sermons. He combines the music and his minister-like approach to the audience in a way that captivates them. Other than the late vocalist Leon Thomas, he is the only other jazz singer who I know uses yodeling as a part of some of his vocal renditions.

A new arrival in Savannah, Cynthia Utterbach, is a breath of fresh air to Savannah's music scene. She refers to herself as the storyteller because she renders very hip dialogue in the midst of her vocal presentations. I have dubbed her "the personification of the American songbook." The lady knows a lot of tunes. Performing with her keeps me on my toes because I never know what to expect on the gig, but I enjoy every minute of it.

Outstanding exceptions

You may wonder why I did not include these two outstanding musicians in my first book, *The Up of the Down Beat* ("Me and the Cats"). There is a very obvious reason. Although they hung out and played with the better musicians, they were inwardly and outwardly two beautiful and very talented ladies. The names Billy Alston and Evelyn Brown may not ring a bell to those who frequented nightclubs and various dances, but "the cats" certainly knew who they were.

Billy Alston was the former wife of saxophonist John "Tiny" Alston (presently the oldest living jazz musician in Savannah). She knew all tunes and never hesitated to share knowledge with young musicians who were serious about learning and playing. She was a regular player on sets and at jam sessions. Billy was also a vocalist who knew lyrics as well as chord changes.

Evelyn Brown was the mother of multi-instrumentalist and vocalist Jimmy Lloyd Brown, leader of the famous soul band Brick. Although Evelyn did not improvise, she was one of the best accompanists that I ever heard or worked with. Like Billy, she knew the standards and played some of the best bass lines on piano that I ever heard. Evelyn was the pianist for Bobby Dilworth and The Blazers band, and the band never used a bass player. Evelyn's sense of time and rhythm was strong to the point that a bass player was neither needed or missed. She was a beautiful and amiable lady who was also willing to teach you if you were serious about learning. They were beautiful ladies but also just as musically hip as the "cats."

"You are here"

You Are Here is an AMC reality series that originally aired during the summer of 2023. Actor, writer, and director Colman Domingo directed the aforementioned reality series that featured four cities that left indelible impression on him: Savannah, Georgia; Philadelphia,

Pennsylvania; New York, New York; and Chicago, Illinois. Savannah was the first one of the features. This program allowed (see email dated May 6) me to share my first serious composition and the inspiration behind it. I, along with the Eric Jones Trio (I frequently use them for accompaniment) and vocalist Huxsie Scott, performed "Her Eyes," inspired by my eldest daughter Tatia (pronounced Tasha). It was overwhelming to know that millions would be watching the series. I could not have asked for better exposure.

Remorse versus fate

One of my most indelible regrets was ultimately countered by fate. I left America in 1968 expecting to return in two years, but it turned out to be almost eleven. I found my utopia in Asia, Tokyo and Bangkok. When I left America, my parents were still a part of the workforce, and my younger siblings were still in high school. When I eventually returned, my younger brother Bobby had served in the military, and my sister Margie was married with a family. "Wow, how time flies." My parents had retired.

Asia was the promised land in a musical sense. Not only was the jazz scene utopian, but I found the love of my life, my wife, Bubpa, and started a family. I didn't realize how selfish I had been until I returned home and witnessed how my family had changed. I was informed by family and friends that although I communicated and sent money home, my absence had taken somewhat of a toll on my parents. I truly regret that.

"God is good." Upon returning home, I was rewarded with the blessing of a reunion of fifteen years with my family and living in the same residence with my parents. They were still in good health most of the time and witnessed my children growing up. Fate can be overwhelmingly rewarding sometimes. In spite of my selfishness, I was blessed by the Almighty.

An unforgettable concert

Johnny Mercer

John Herndon Mercer (Johnny Mercer, November 19, 1909–June 25, 1976) was born in Savannah, Georgia, and is perhaps its most famous music artist. Although not a jazz artist, two factors created leverage for imputing the jazz genre to his reputation. His collaborations with Duke Ellington (Satin Doll) and Lionel Hampton (Midnight Sun) produced songs that became both jazz and popular standards. Johnny's vast number of lyricized popular songs not only earned him four Academy Awards and numerous Golden Globe Awards and Grammies, but they also became a part of the American Songbook and have been incorporated into the jazz genre as evidenced by jazz artists playing and recording them.

In the summer of 1993, the Coastal Jazz Association (now Savannah Jazz) presented a memorable fundraising concert at the estate of Johnny Mercer located on *Moon River*. It was an indelible evening of outstanding jazz. The event was held outdoors overlooking the river, and a special band was chosen to perform some of Johnny's many songs: yours truly, Ben Tucker, Ben Riley, Gina Rene, and nationally acclaimed pianist Ray Gallon. The food was the best of Southern cuisine, and the weather was perfect. It was an evening that I, as well as those in attendance, will not forget.

My first real challenge in music

It seems as if it was just a short while ago, but it has been more than sixty years. I was a senior in high school when my band director, Mr. La'Roy Miller, said to me one day, "Teddy, I think I can get you a full scholarship at Florida A&M University (FAMU) if you want it and can pass the audition." Now, that was music to my ears because it was he who had introduced our high school band to FAMU. He had taken our high school band to see them perform four times during my senior year.

After that conversation, I practiced diligently every day and night. He and a friend took me to Tallahassee, Florida, early on a Saturday morning. The audition was scheduled for 11:00 a.m., and I could not have been more apprehensive. When we arrived at the band room on time, we were greeted by the band director, Dr. Foster, and his assistant, Dr. Leonard Bowie. Shortly after that, an older short gray-haired gentleman approached me and introduced himself as Leo Bowden, director of lower brass.

I felt that I was prepared for the audition, and his amicable demeanor put me more at ease. Although the butterflies did surface and I was mildly critiqued regarding some areas, alternate positions and breathing, I received a high Pass rating and was awarded the scholarship.

To date, I regard that as one of my most rewarding accomplishments. Unfortunately, I did not attend FAMU when I graduated from high school. Hanging out, gigging, and having fun at that time outweighed my education, and I eventually opted to join the US Air Force in an attempt to see the world. College would come much later, but I still cherish that experience.

A spiritual experience

I remember an unforgettable spiritual/musical experience that happened in Bessemer, Alabama, a suburb of Birmingham. I was attending a jazz forum hosted by trumpeter, pianist, and educator Jothan Callins ("Me and the Cats," *The Up of the Down Beat*).

Included at the forum were Donald Byrd, Larry Ridley, Consuela Lee, Tommy Stewart, Ed Nelson, Nelson Harrison, Carl Atkins, Ike Carter, and several other dedicated musicians and advocates. It lasted three days and was entitled Jazz Reparation. The intent was to challenge the underappreciation of the art form called jazz and place it in its appropriate position as being one of the quintessential and profound art forms in the world.

The forum was a stimulating and heartfelt attempt to do something about an art form that has been and is still being denied proper recognition as one of America's gifts to the world. Various discussions, proposals, and ideas were pondered with the intent of eventual implementation. Unfortunately, Jothan Callins, who spearheaded the effort, died before success was accomplished.

For three days, we debated and proposed various ideas. We hung out and broke bread together and had some incredible jam sessions. One of the sessions was held at Jothan's brother's house. He has a very nice place with a large yard, swimming pool, and den (with a tuned piano) and served some of the best Southern cuisine that I have ever tasted. However, the epiphany of the evening was realizing what we already knew and had somehow all but forgotten.

Jothan's mother was asked to join the jam session, and she, with hesitation, did join but chose to sing an old church spiritual. It had the rhythm commonly found in the Baptist or Pentecostal churches. Man, she grooved it, and we joined in and raised the groove to incredible heights. Everyone simultaneously realized what was happening musically, and we had a ball playing that song.

That experience is indelible, and I really witnessed the meaning of *Call and Response*. All of us experienced the Holy Spirit and fully understood jazz being a derivative of the church music experience.

A pleasant and unexpected surprise

Me and the Savannah Philharmonic Symphony's
conductor Keitaro Harada

I had the pleasure and privilege of performing with the Savannah Philharmonic Orchestra at its annual 2023 Christmas Concert. The concert was the imaginative, eclectic, and entertaining effort of violinist extraordinaire Ricardo Ochoa. I was impressed with his production as well as the orchestrations done by fellow musicians Eric Jones and Marc Chesanow.

I knew that the conductor Keitaro Harada was from Japan but did not know that he had been the Associate Conductor for the Tokyo Symphony Orchestra. Meeting him for the first time and sharing with him that I had lived and performed in Japan for almost eleven years with the majority of the time spent in Tokyo surprised him, and I was also surprised that although he is a classical musician and a lot younger than I, he has an affinity for jazz and either knew or had heard of everyone whom I had played with.

Not only was I impressed with his appreciation for jazz, but I was more impressed with his conducting and interpretative skills. Meeting and performing with him was an incredible experience. Life and encounters are like syncopation in music. Things happen when you least expect them, yet they are an enhancement of both music and also life's journey. As it has often been stated, "It's a small world isn't it?"

The Future of Jazz

Me and mentees, Jaron McCarr, Robert Stringer, Andre Murchison

I have been very fortunate for the past twelve years to present a program aptly entitled "The Future of Jazz." This privilege is made possible during black history month as a result of a grant administered to the Black Heritage Festival from the City of Savannah. The festival is under the auspices of Savannah State University.

The grant allows me to select students ranging from middle school to the college level and feature them in concert to the general public free of charge. Most of the students are aspiring jazz musicians, and some of them are inherently talented students in pursuit of other careers, but all of them can be considered precocious. They represent schools from Georgia, Florida, South Carolina, and Alabama and are selected by the music teachers and/or band directors.

A full day of rehearsing coupled with a masterclass or workshop held by me and other professional musicians help enlighten and prepare them for an evening concert. The students must be able to read and improvise at a very high level.

This experience is very rewarding and informative. The students share camaraderie and engage in friendly but challenging competition. The music played is as equally challenging as the competition. The culmination of this experience always wows the audience and gives the participants a sense of satisfaction and accomplishment.

This musical experience is equally rewarding to me. I am able to compose, arrange, teach, and reap the benefit of having my music played and interpreted on a level that is almost commensurate to professional musicians. These kids are really something else. Although all the participants are impressive, some of them stand out above the rest. The following list reflects aspiring artists who have embraced the jazz world with promising success:

Jamison Ross, drums
Robert Boone, drums
T. J. Reddick, drums
Alphonso Horne, trumpet
Andrae Murchison, trombone
Morgan Guerin, saxophones, piano, drums, bass
Jalen Baker, vibraphone
Amina Scott, bass

In the Trenches

The advocation, perception, and support of this great art form commonly referred to as jazz is absolutely necessary for it to exist and allow its creators, the musicians/artists, to continue pursuing and exploring musical possibilities. Although the artists are responsible for creating, those individuals who advocate and fight for them to perpetuate their creations and the art form deserve credit.

People like Ron Flagg and his wife, Tana, work tirelessly supporting this great art form. I'm sure that this responsibility was imputed to Tana by Ron. However, Ron grew up in a jazz-supportive environment. His father was a jazz enthusiast and befriended many jazz musicians. According to Ron, musicians were always in and out of their home in Jamaica, New York. His father befriended trumpeter Cootie Williams (of Duke Ellington Orchestra fame) and helped care for his wife. After their demise, Ron's father received royalties from his estate, and Ron still receives them now. No wonder we can count on him when we need him.

Ruth Keith, a long-time Savannah Jazz member, has been the secretary, supporter, and volunteer for seventeen years and can always be depended upon when needed. Paula Fogarty, executive director of Savannah Jazz, is dependable, creative, knowledgeable, and devoted to the organization and art form. She is only the second person to serve as its director. It's hard to imagine her not being at the helm. I compare her to the well-known Energizer Bunny. She keeps on ticking. Proof positive is reflected in the successful completion of the Savannah Jazz History and Hall of Fame Exhibit, covered earlier in this book. What would we do without you, Paula?

Tanya Milton, with a long career in advertising and the present editor of the *Savannah Tribune*, a weekly newspaper that is free to the general public, can be counted upon for her support and advocacy. Richard "Skip" Jennings, Savannah Jazz board member emeritus, has always been a strong supporter of jazz and still works with the Savannah Jazz artist committee. Skip served as the master of ceremonies for the jazz festival for thirty-five years and still makes periodic appearances. You are sure to catch him on Blues night at the festival. It could be because he books all of the festival's blues acts. Yeah, that's it.

Colin Schofield is currently the president of Savannah Jazz as well as Jody Jazz (saxophone mouthpiece manufactory). He is a dedicated leader and true jazz enthusiast. From what I have seen thus far, great things are expected under his leadership. Another of our devoted board of directors members is Jim Carswell, who heads the team of SPYHOP Productions, creating television programming, broadcast news, and branded content. He was managing editor/news anchor at WTOC-TV for eleven years and served in the same capacity at WSAV-TV for six years.

Jim brings a wealth of knowledge and expertise and can be relied upon for advice direction in both media and advertising concerns. Jim also serves as master of ceremonies for the Savannah Jazz annual festivals and other events. He is a welcomed and appreciated asset.

Tom Glaser is one of the "founding fathers" of Savannah Jazz (formerly the Coastal Jazz Association) and its first president. Although relocating and retiring in the Atlanta area, he never lost contact and, upon returning to Savannah, resumed his posture as an advocate, financial supporter, and board of directors member. He can be trusted to do whatever is needed to preserve the art form of jazz. He is a member of the Savannah Jazz Hall of Fame and currently at the helm of the Savannah Jazz education committee.

Two of Savannah's mayors have been quite instrumental in keeping jazz alive in Savannah. Former two-term mayor Otis Johnson is a dedicated jazz advocate and has always been one. Because of his long-standing involvement, he has been indicted into the Savannah Jazz Hall of Fame and currently serves on its education committee.

Current two-term mayor Van Johnson is maintaining the same posture and can be relied upon to do whatever he can to perpetuate the city's jazz legacy. It was he who appointed yours truly as Savannah's first official Ambassador of Jazz. What a blessing to have this level of support from Savannah's top officials. A million thanks, Honorable Ones, for all you do and have done. It's because of you that Savannah is in a good place regarding the most profound music art form in existence, the art form commonly referred to as jazz.

The Beat Goes On

Now in the twilight of my life and nearing the end of this incredible musical journey, I have no regrets about embarking upon it. Sure, there are a lot of things I would do differently if it was possible to take another trip, knowing that it's not. The experiences that I have had and shared, the people I have encountered, and the happiness that I have experienced comprise a reciprocal process.

Over the years, I have fully comprehended that music is a universal language, and jazz more than any other genre has spoken in a manner that is unequalled by any other music. Musicians, the creators of this great art form, are special individuals. Some of them realized their spirituality, and some wrestled with demons, but they always loved, created, and perpetuated the art form. As previously and often stated, the art form referred to as jazz is unequivocally the most profound music art form in existence, yet it is certainly the most underappreciated genre of all the existing genres of music.

This great art form has permeated the entire world, and even when not understood, listeners realize that it offers something that is special and different. During my travels, I have in many places observed a greater appreciation for jazz than the place where it was created, America. I sometimes ponder and wonder if the lack of appreciation in America is motivated because of its true and original creators. I would like to believe that this possibility is not true.

On a positive note, the art form has finally been accepted in the academic arena. Major institutions of higher learning are now including jazz curriculums as offered majors. Outstanding specialized jazz conservatories are nationwide, and some local school systems now have magnet music programs with a jazz concentration or focus. Unlike the original creators and pioneers, most musicians today have been formerly trained. It is understood if a youngster chooses a career in jazz, he or she must decide on a music school to attend as any other professional career pursuer.

In 1987, the US Congress declared jazz a national treasure. Although it is a twentieth-century art form, it's America's only indigenous art form, yet still it has not received its just due. This writer during this long musical journey, 1956 to the present, has done everything within my power to elevate and perpetuate this special art form. Along the way, I have encountered many individuals who understand, support, and advocate for its existence—surely not enough but certainly better than none.

I hope to live long enough to witness jazz appreciation and elevation to its well-deserved and rightful place among the art forms of the world. There are a few of us who know the truth, and hopefully you, the listeners and readers, will wake up and realize its profoundness and importance.

Epilogue

In the hushed corridors of jazz history, there are certain names that resonate with a unique resonance, echoing through the gravity of time like a timeless melody. Among these luminaries stands Teddy Adams—a titan of rhythm, a maestro of the soul, and a guardian of the art form commonly known as jazz.

As a sequel to *The Up of the Down Beat* and the final pages of *Keepin' the Beat*, we find ourselves not at the end of a jazz musician's well-lived life but rather at the beginning of a legacy—a legacy that Dr. Teddy Adams has spent a lifetime shaping and nurturing with the care and dedication of a master craftsman. As he drew inspiration from stories of his life and the rhythms of the world around him, *Keepin' the Beat* is his magnum opus.

Through the pages of his memoirs, we've journeyed with Teddy through the smoky clubs and bustling cities of Tokyo, Japan, and Moscow, Russia, to the back alleys and cobbled stoned streets of Savannah, Georgia, where the sounds of jazz reverberate through the night air like a Southern mother's call when streetlights illuminate at sunset. We've felt the pulse of jazz through the heartbeat of his soul and the spirit of improvisation and innovation.

But more than just a chronicle of his own remarkable journey, *Keepin' the Beat* is a testament to Teddy's unwavering commitment to preserving and perpetuating the legacy of jazz. From his early days as a young musician finding his voice in the vibrant jazz scene of the 1950s to his role as a mentor and educator shaping the next generation of talent, Teddy's influence extends far beyond the confines of any stage, studio, or lecture hall.

As we close the book on Teddy's memoir, we are left with a profound sense of gratitude for his contributions to the world of music and to the countless lives he has touched along the way. His passion, perseverance, and unyielding belief in the power of jazz serve as a beacon of inspiration for us all.

And so, as we bid farewell to these pages, let us remember Dr. Teddy Adams not only as a virtuoso of the trombone but also as a guardian of a tradition, a keeper of the flame, and a true embodiment of the timeless spirit of jazz. For in his music, in his words, and in his legacy, he carries the weight of a lifetime's worth of melodies and memories through the art form formally known as jazz.

As the city of Savannah evolves and grows, jazz remains a constant. Teddy's legacy reminds us of our shared humanity and the power of music to transcend barriers and unite hearts. His journey inspires us all for a harmonious future and to continue *keepin' the beat.*

my daughter, Tatia Adams Fox

About the Author

Teddy Adams is a multifaceted artist who wears many hats. He is a trombonist, composer, lecturer, and educator. Originally from Savannah, Georgia, he has traveled and performed locally, regionally, nationally, and internationally. Some of his performances and recordings include many of jazz's biggest names such as Art Blakey, Rufus Reid, Ben Riley, Ben Tucker, Delbert Felix, Abbey Lincoln, Irene Reid, Wycliffe Gordon, Cab Calloway, Doug Carn, and James Moody, and the list goes on and on.

Teddy is a charter member of the Savannah Jazz Hall of Fame and one of the cofounders of the Coastal Jazz Association (now Savannah Jazz Association), the Savannah Jazz Festival, and the Annual Christmas Concert and Jam Session now approaching its forty-seventh year. He has performed at all of the Savannah Jazz Festivals and several times at other festivals that include Piccolo Spoleto, Gullah, Atlanta, Jacksonville, and many others. Teddy has also been the recipient of many awards that include The Key to the City of Savannah and recently being appointed Savannah's first Official Jazz Ambassador by Mayor Van Johnson. He has also authored his book, *The Up of the Down Beat*, and is in the process of writing a sequel/legacy, *Keepin' the Beat*.

Teddy, along with Randy Reese, is the cofounder of the Savannah Jazz Orchestra. He presently leads several small groups, which include the Teddy Adams Sextet. In addition to serving in the US Air Force for ten years and retiring after a thirty-four-year career with the city of Savannah, he is presently teaching in the music department of Savannah State University and has served as music director for Savannah's premier jazz club, Good Times Jazz Bar and Restaurant, since its opening almost five years ago.

Printed in the USA
CPSIA information can be obtained
at www.ICGtesting.com
LVHW071443151024
793861LV00015B/224/J